GRAMMAR
FOR GREAT WRITING

B

SERIES CONSULTANT:
KEITH S. FOLSE

DEBORAH GORDON

BARBARA SMITH-PALINKAS

NATIONAL GEOGRAPHIC LEARNING | **CENGAGE Learning**

Australia • Brazil • Mexico • Singapore • United Kingdom • United States

Grammar for Great Writing:
Student Book B, **First Edition**
Deborah Gordon • Barbara Smith-Palinkas

Publisher: Sherrise Roehr

Executive Editor: Laura Le Dréan

Senior Development Editor: Jennifer Bixby

Media Researcher: Leila Hishmeh

Senior Technology Product Manager: Scott Rule

Director of Global Marketing: Ian Martin

Product Marketing Manager: Dalia Bravo

Sr. Director, ELT & World Languages: Michael Burggren

Production Manager: Daisy Sosa

Content Project Manager: Beth Houston

Senior Print Buyer: Mary Beth Hennebury

Composition: SPI-Global

Cover/Text Design: Brenda Carmichael

Art Director: Brenda Carmichael

Cover Image: ©dtokar/Getty Images

Sunrise over the Dead Sea lights up little salt islands in Jordan.

For product information and technology assistance, contact us at **Cengage Learning Customer & Sales Support, cengage.com/contact**

For permission to use material from this text or product, submit all requests online at **cengage.com/permissions**
Further permissions questions can be emailed to **permissionrequest@cengage.com**

Student Edition:
ISBN: 978-1-337-11860-6

National Geographic Learning
20 Channel Center Street
Boston, MA 02210
USA

National Geographic Learning, a Cengage Learning Company, has a mission to bring the world to the classroom and the classroom to life. With our English language programs, students learn about their world by experiencing it. Through our partnerships with National Geographic and TED, they develop the language and skills they need to be successful global citizens and leaders.

Locate your local office at **international.cengage.com/region**

Visit National Geographic Learning online at **NGL.cengage.com/ELT**
Visit our corporate website at **www.cengage.com**

Printed in the United States of America
Print Number: 01 Print Year: 2017

Contents

Scope and Sequence

Unit	Common Errors	Vocabulary in Academic Writing	Kinds of Writing
1 **Writing about the Present**	1.1 Does the verb agree with the subject? 1.2 Do you need simple present or present progressive? 1.3 Do you need simple present or present perfect?	*Verbs Frequently Used in Simple Present* argue define indicate believe illustrate require change increase show come	Descriptive: *Choosing a Major* Descriptive: *The Human Heart*
2 **Writing about the Past**	2.1 Is the simple past form correct? 2.2 Is the past progressive form correct? 2.3 Do you need simple past or past progressive? 2.4 Are verb tenses consistent?	*Verbs Frequently Used in the Past* be do say become have take begin make work come	Descriptive: *The Pax Romana* Narrative: *The Beginning of World War I*
3 **Writing with the Present Perfect**	3.1 Do you need simple present or present perfect? 3.2 Do you need simple past or present perfect?	*Verbs Frequently Used in Present Perfect* be give see become have show come make take do	Introductory: *Global Warming* Cause-Effect: *Murray College*
4 **Writing about the Future**	4.1 Is the correct verb form used after *will* or *may*? 4.2 Do you need to use *will* or *may*? 4.3 Does the clause need a future or present verb?	*Verbs Frequently Used in the Future* be go know become happen lead come have need do	Introductory: *Ethnography Proposal* Process: *Project Proposal*
5 **Writing with Prepositions**	5.1 Is the preposition correct? 5.2 Does the verb after a prepositional phrase agree with the subject? 5.3 Is the preposition combination correct?	*Frequently Used Adjective + Preposition Combinations* associated with different from responsible aware of interested in for capable of known as similar to concerned about related to	Cause-Effect: *An Apple a Day* Comparison: *How Cultures View Aging*
6 **Using Modals in Sentences**	6.1 Does the modal need *to*? 6.2 Is the negative form correct? 6.3 Do you hedge correctly?	*Frequently Used Modal + Verb Combinations* can help might seem should try to could do must take will continue to be have to should include would be may lead to	Opinion: *The Best Age for Children to Learn to Read* Opinion: *The Future of Money*
7 **Using Adjective Clauses**	7.1 Do you use *which*, *who*, or *that*? 7.2 Does the adjective clause need a comma? 7.3 Does the adjective clause have a subject pronoun? 7.4 Is there an extra object pronoun?	*Words from the Academic Word List (Sublists 4 and 5)* access conflicts precise adequate exposure prior alter phases trends challenge	Descriptive: *Eduardo Kobra* Definition: *Shinichi Suzuki*
8 **Writing with Adverb Clauses**	8.1 Is there a comma missing? 8.2 Is it a fragment? 8.3 Does each clause have a subject and a verb? 8.4 Is there an extra connector?	*Words from the Academic Word List (Sublists 4 and 5)* concentration hypothesis labels debate implications obvious emerge investigations options goals	Descriptive: *Multitasking* Narrative: *Frogtown*

Unit	Common Errors	Vocabulary in Academic Writing	Kinds of Writing
9 **Writing with Articles**	9.1 Is the article *a* or *an* missing? 9.2 Is the article *the* missing? 9.3 Are you making a general or specific reference? 9.4 Is an article used where one is not needed?	*Frequently Used Nouns* education number result example participants studies health research variety increase	Classification: *Types of Long-Term Memory* Cause-Effect: *Becoming an Everyday Environmentalist*
10 **Writing Simple and Compound Sentences**	10.1 Does the independent clause have a subject and a verb? 10.2 Is a comma missing? 10.3 Is a coordinating conjunction missing?	*Words from the Academic Word List (Sublists 5 and 6)* aware fundamental ratio capacity generation version decline notion whereas equivalent	Problem-Solution: *Sleeping Cold* Comparison: *Cultural Interpretations of Facial Expressions*
11 **Using Parallel Structure**	11.1 Are items parallel before and after a conjunction? 11.2 Are items after each part of a correlative conjunction parallel? 11.3 Are items in a comparison parallel?	*Words from the Academic Word List (Sublist 6)* accurate exceed intelligence author fees migration brief gender revealed enhanced	Descriptive: *Thatched Roofs in England* Classification: *Levels of Airline Service*
12 **Using Passive Voice**	12.1 Is the passive missing a form of *be*? 12.2 Is the passive form correct? 12.3 Do you need passive or active voice?	*Frequently Used Passive Verb Forms* are based is needed were asked can be seen was made were conducted can be used was reported were found is known	Cause-Effect: *Headaches in Children* Classification: *Elements of an Effective Apology*
13 **Using Gerunds and Infinitives**	13.1 Is the verb followed by an infinitive or a gerund? 13.2 Is the correct form used after a preposition? 13.3 Is the subject a gerund? 13.4 Is there a subject? 13.5 Is there a singular verb after a gerund or infinitive subject?	*Verbs Frequently Used after Gerunds or Infinitives* be know participate develop learn use find make work have	Process: *Saving Wildlife* Process: *Finding More Time*
14 **Writing with Noun Clauses**	14.1 Is the word order correct? 14.2 Is the verb form correct? 14.3 Is a question word or *that*-phrase missing? 14.4 Is the noun clause missing a subject or verb?	*Verbs Frequently Used with Noun Clauses* be prefer serve do remember show feel report suggest find	Narrative: *The Mysterious Key* Descriptive: *Recognizing the Sleep-Deprived*
15 **Using Connectors for Better Writing**	15.1 Is there an extra connector? 15.2 Is the connector correct? 15.3 Is a connector missing? 15.4 Is punctuation missing or incorrect?	*Verbs Frequently Used with Connectors* be make state can recognize suggest do should take have	Classification: *Forest Biomes* Comparison: *How Learning a Foreign Language Has Changed*

Overview

ABOUT THE *GRAMMAR FOR GREAT WRITING* SERIES

Grammar for Great Writing is a three-book series that helps students with the specific grammar they actually need to strengthen their academic writing. Activities feature academic vocabulary and content, providing clear models for good academic writing. Ideal for the grammar component of a writing and grammar class, *Grammar for Great Writing* may be used as a companion to the *Great Writing* series or in conjunction with any academic writing textbook.

This series consists of three levels: A, B, and C.

Book A is for low intermediate students and is designed to complement the writing and grammar found in *Great Writing 2*.

Book B is for intermediate students and is designed to complement the writing and grammar found in *Great Writing 3*.

Book C is for upper intermediate to advanced students and is designed to complement the writing and grammar found in *Great Writing 4*.

ORGANIZATION

Each of the three books in this series consists of 15 units, and each unit focuses solidly on one area of grammar that causes problems for ESL and EFL writers. These 45 grammar points have been selected based on input from experienced English language teachers and student writers. Although many grammar points appear in only one book, others are so important that they appear in more than one book. Students work with the grammar point in increasingly more complex sentences and rhetorical modes as they progress through the different levels of the series.

The units have been carefully designed so that they may be taught in any order. In fact, it is possible to skip units if teachers believe that a particular grammar point is not problematic for their students. In other words, teachers should review the table of contents, which calls out the common student errors addressed in each unit, and carefully choose which of the 15 grammar topics to present and in which order.

CONTENTS OF A UNIT

Each of the six sections in a unit contains presentation and practice. Although each unit has a specific grammatical focus, the following sections appear in every unit:

What Do You Know?

This opening activity is designed to grab the students' attention and help them assess their understanding of the grammar point. *What Do You Know* has two parts. First students are directed to look at the unit opening photo and think about how it is related to the topic of the paragraph. They discuss two questions related to the photo that are designed to elicit use of the target grammar. Then students read the paragraph that has two common errors in it. The paragraph has a clear rhetorical style. Students work together to find the grammar errors and explain the corrections.

Grammar Forms

Clear charts present and explain the form of the unit's grammar focus. Follow-up activities focus students' attention on the grammar form.

Common Uses

How the grammar is used in writing is a unique part of the series. The common use charts explain how the grammar point is actually used in academic writing. A follow-up activity provides practice.

Common Errors

Here students are presented with a series of two to five of the most common errors that student writers typically make with the unit grammar point. The focus is on errors found in academic writing, and each error chart is followed by an activity.

Academic Vocabulary

Academic vocabulary is a unique feature of this series. Using corpus and frequency data, we have identified vocabulary that most naturally combines with the grammar focus of the unit. The *Vocabulary in Academic Writing* activity presents items from a broad range of academic subject areas.

Put It Together

The *Review Quiz* gives teachers a chance to quickly check how much students have learned about forming and using the grammar point. In this short activity of only eight items, students answer five multiple-choice questions and then identify and correct errors in three items.

In *Building Greater Sentences*, students combine three or more short sentences into one coherent sentence that uses the target grammar structure.

Steps to Composing is an engaging and interactive activity in which students read a paragraph consisting of 8 to 12 sentences. The paragraph models a specific rhetorical style. While none of the sentences contain outright errors, the writing can be improved. To this end, there are 10 steps that instruct the student in how to improve the sentences. Most of the time the instructions are very specific (for example, combine sentences 2 and 3 with the word *because*). Other times they are intentionally more open in order to challenge the student (for example, add a descriptive adjective to the sentence).

Finally, *Original Writing* consists of a writing assignment connected to the grammar topic, focusing on a specific rhetorical style of writing. There are three example sentences to give the student ideas for a topic. The amount of writing that is required will depend on the student, the teacher, and the objectives for the course.

Acknowledgements

I am grateful to the many people who have worked so hard on the development and production of *Grammar for Great Writing*, including Laura Le Dréan and Jennifer Bixby of National Geographic Learning, authors Deborah Gordon and Barbara Smith-Palinkas, and contributing editor Lise Minovitz. Ultimately, everyone's ideas and feedback have been instrumental in the design of this work.

I would also like to acknowledge the input from the thousands of ESL and EFL students that I have taught throughout my teaching career. *Grammar for Great Writing* is the result of many years of teaching academic writing to students all over the world. This series is very much based on learner needs, particularly grammar problems that I have seen students struggle with as they are trying to improve their academic writing in English. These classroom experiences have been instrumental in shaping which grammar is covered as well as how it is presented and practiced.

Finally, many thanks to the following reviewers who offered important ideas and helpful suggestions that shaped the *Grammar for Great Writing* series:

Nancy Boyer, Golden West College, California

Tony Carnerie, University of California, San Diego Language Institute, California

Angela Cox, Spring International Language Center, Arkansas

Luke Daly, Harold Washington College, Illinois

Rachel Dictor, DePaul University English Language Academy, Illinois

Ian Dreilinger, Center for Multilingual Multicultural Studies, Florida

Edward Feighny, Houston Community College, Texas

Timothy Fojtik, Concordia University Wisconsin, Wisconsin

Janile Hill, DePaul University English Language Academy, Illinois

Elizabeth Kelley, University of California, San Diego Language Institute, California

Toby Killcreas, Auburn University at Montgomery, Alabama

Lisa Kovacs, University of California, San Diego Language Institute, California

Maria Lerma, Orange Coast College, California

Wendy McBride, University of Arkansas, Spring International Language Center, Arkansas

Kathy Najafi, Houston Community College, Texas

Anne Politz, Drexel University, Pennsylvania

Wendy Ramer, Broward Community College, Florida

Helen Roland, Miami Dade College, Florida

Kody Salzburn, Auburn University at Montgomery, Alabama

Gail Schwartz, University of California, Irvine, California

Karen Shock, Savannah College of Art and Design, Georgia

Adriana Treadway, Spring International Language Center, Arkansas

Anne McGee Tyoan, Savannah College of Art and Design, Georgia

—*Keith S. Folse*

Series Consultant

Photo Credits

Cover: dtokar/E+/Getty Images.

02–03 JOEL SARTORE/National Geographic Creative, **10** (b) Nikolaev Mikhail/Shutterstock.com, **13** (t) Matt of Florence/500Px, **16-17** Gjon Mili/The LIFE Picture Collection/Getty Images, **29** (t) Frans Lanting/National Geographic Creative, **32-33** Paolo Pellegrin/Magnum Photos, **41** (t) John Warburton Lee/Superstock, **44-45** AAron Ontiveroz/Getty Images, **55** (t) Mark Peterson/Redux Pictures, **58-59** Catherine Karnow/National Geographic Creative, **61** (b) Robert Clark/National Geographic Creative, **69** (t) Stas Moroz/Shutterstock.com, **72-73** 2004 LYNN JOHNSON/National Geographic Image Collection, **83** (t) Darios/Shutterstock.com, **86-87** YASUYOSHI CHIBA/AFP/Getty Images, **90** (b) STEVE RAYMER/National Geographic Creative, **97** (t) Standret/Shutterstock.com, **100-101** Ian Trower/Alamy Stock Photo, **103** (bc) PHIL SCHERMEISTER/National Geographic Creative, **111** (t) Angel DiBilio/Shutterstock.com, **114-115** MAGGIE STEBER/National Geographic Creative, **124** (b) Hero Images/Getty Images, **127** (t) Welcomia/Shutterstock.com, **130-131** Gary Hershorn/REUTERS, **141** (t) Steve Dunwell/Photolibrary/Getty Images, **144-145** Peter Cavanagh/Alamy Stock Photo, **152** (b) DAVID ALAN HARVEY/National Geographic Creative, **155** (t) Andrzej Kubik/Shutterstock.com, **158-159** EMILY BERL/The New York Times/Redux Pictures, **169** (t) JOEL SARTORE/National Geographic Creative, **172-173** AMI VITALE/National Geographic Creative, **183** (tl) Kim Kyung Hoon/Reuters, **186-187** DEA/A. DAGLI ORTI/De Agostini Picture Library/Getty Images, **189** (b) mavo/Shutterstock.com, **197** (t) Andrew Aitchison/Corbis Historical/Getty Images, **200-201** JODY MACDONALD/National Geographic Creative, **204** (b) TINO SORIANO/National Geographic Creative, **213** (t) Tim Hale Photography/Corbis/Getty Images.

References

Biber, D., et al. (1999). *Longman grammar of spoken and written English*. New York: Longman.

Coxhead, A. (2000). See http://www.victoria.ac.nz/lals/resources/academicwordlist/

Davies, M. (2008–). *The corpus of contemporary American English: 520 million words, 1990–present*. Available at http://corpus.byu.edu/coca/

Student biologists look for the endangered smoky madtom, a species of catfish.

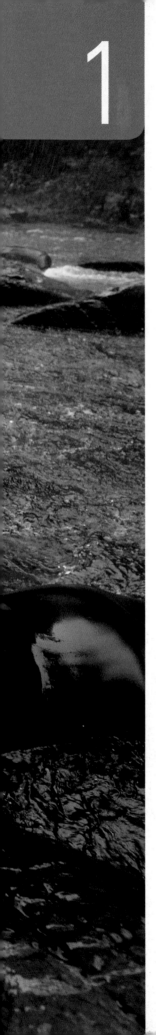

1 Writing about the Present

WHAT DO YOU KNOW?

DISCUSS Look at the photo and read the caption. Discuss the questions.

1. Do students in your school conduct research outside of class? If so, what kind of research do students do?

2. How can conducting research help a student choose a major?

FIND THE ERRORS This paragraph contains two errors with present or present progressive verbs. Find the errors and correct them. Explain your corrections to a partner.

DESCRIPTIVE PARAGRAPH

Choosing a Major

[1] Many students in their first year of university study has difficulty choosing majors. [2] Fortunately, there are some steps students can take to help them make the right choice. [3] First, students can meet with an academic advisor. [4] Because academic advisors are familiar with all the majors offered at the university, they are providing helpful information to guide students toward a specific field of study. [5] Next, students can visit the university career center and meet with a career advisor. [6] Career advisors are knowledgeable about the type of major needed for a specific career. [7] Career advisors also administer skills inventories and career interest tests to help students identify possible careers. [8] Finally, students can ask their professors for advice. [9] Professors are able to share their experiences and offer valuable insights into what studying a specific major requires in terms of skills, abilities, and effort. [10] After taking these steps, students are usually ready to select a major in their second year of academic study.

Grammar Forms

1.1 Simple Present

Subject	Verb	Example
I / you / we / they	verb	Environmental engineers **work** on the protection of the environment and human health.
he / she / it	verb + -s	The government agency **wants** nuclear testing to continue as planned.

1.2 Present Form of *Be*

Subject	Verb	Example
I	*am*	I **am** a citizen of both Spain and Colombia.
he / she / it	*is*	The company's main office **is** in Rome.
you / we / they	*are*	Strong teachers **are** essential for preparing students for higher education.

1.3 Present Progressive

Subject	Verb	Example
I	*am* + verb + *-ing*	With this research, I **am attempting** to prove the effectiveness of the new medication.
he / she / it	*is* + verb + *-ing*	Panama **is building** a larger canal.
we / you / they	*are* + verb + *-ing*	Because of the weak economy, small businesses **are growing** very slowly.

1.4 Present Perfect

Subject	Verb	Example
I / you / we / they	*have* + past participle	The Csango people **have lived** in Romania's Moldova region for over a thousand years.
he / she / it	*has* + past participle	Russian pianist Yevgeny Kissin **has given** concerts since he was a child.

Notes

1. Contractions are almost never used in academic writing.
2. See Appendix 4, Irregular Verbs, on page 220 for examples of irregular past participles.

1.5 Negative Present Forms

Form	Examples
do / does not + base form of the verb	This article reports on one business that **does not have** any employees.
be + not	Many workers **are not** comfortable in their jobs.
be + not + verb + *-ing*	The main researcher for NASA's mission to Mars **is not planning** to visit the planet.
have / has + not + past participle	The Himalayan mountain climbers **have not seen** their families since late last year.

Note

Contractions with *not* are rare in academic writing.

ACTIVITY 1

Fill in the blank with the correct form of the verb in parentheses: simple present, present progressive, or present perfect. Use *not* when it is given.

1. The earth _____ (*become, present progressive*) warmer, so scientists are worried about the future of the planet.

2. Aircraft mechanics _____ (*wear, simple present*) headphones at work because the planes are so loud.

3. The documentary on pollution _____ (*receive, present progressive*) a lot of attention from critics.

4. The volunteers _____ (*not, travel, present perfect*) since the war began.

5. I _____ (*preview, simple present*) upcoming chapters before the instructor's lecture, and it always makes me more prepared for class.

6. The latest legislation _____ (*not, help, present progressive*) students with their huge college loans.

7. The indigenous tribes _____ (*want, always, present perfect*) a land of their own.

8. The singer _____ (*be, present*) also a well-known environmental activist.

Common Uses

1.6 Using Simple Present

The simple present is commonly used in academic writing. It is used:

1. to write about general truths and facts that are not limited to a specific time	It **takes** about 12 hours for your body to digest a meal.
2. to write about a repeated or habitual action	Every fall, Canadian geese **fly** south for the winter.
3. to cite a source	Sleep researchers **say** that most people dream four to six times per night.
4. to give details about information from a book, poem, or film • We use simple present because an event in a book or film remains the same every time we read or see it. This is called the literary present.	In "The Story of an Hour," Mrs. Mallard **learns** of her husband's death, but she **does not feel** sad.

Note

Stative (non-action) verbs describe a state, rather than an action. They usually take the simple present form of the verb. Note the most common ones below.

be (exist)	consist of	dislike	realize	seem	want
belong to	depend on	include	recognize	understand	

1.7 Using Present Progressive

The present progressive is not as commonly used in writing as other verb forms. However, it is used:

1. to describe events in real time	In some countries, people **are paying** more taxes than ever before.
2. to write about the continuation of an event	Temperatures **are continuing** to rise because of global warming.

1.8 Using Present Perfect

The present perfect is used to write about past events that are still relevant now. It is used:

1. to write about an event that happened in the past and continues until now • Use *since* with a specific date or time. Use *for* with a period of time.	Alaska **has been** a U.S. state **since** 1959. Alaska **has been** a U.S. state **for** more than 50 years.
2. to write about a very recent past event that is important to the current discussion	The government **has passed** a new tax law that will have an immediate impact on citizens.

ACTIVITY 2

Fill in the blank with the correct simple present, present progressive, or present perfect form of the verb in parentheses. Use *not* when given. More than one answer may be possible.

1. In his poem "The Raven," author Edgar Allen Poe _____ (*use*) numerous symbols to express loneliness.

2. Global sea levels _____ (*rise*) rapidly since the beginning of the 21st century.

3. Historians _____ (*begin*) to study some alternative causes of World War I.

4. Unfortunately, people from developing countries _____ (*not, have*) the same opportunities as those in wealthier nations to start small businesses.

5. In that country, government regulations _____ (*not, allow*) politicians to accept contributions from private companies.

6. As governments spend more money on cancer research, medical professionals _____ (*conduct*) more extensive studies on possible cures.

7. Because people's desire to explore space is stronger than ever, astronomers _____ (*work*) on a new super telescope.

8. In his book *The Art of Happiness*, the Dalai Lama _____ (*state*) that we can train in happiness much like we can train in any other skill.

Common Errors

Common Error 1.1 Does the verb agree with the subject?

speak
The people of Northern Africa ~~speaks~~ French, Arabic, and some Italian.

is
The family ~~are~~ emigrating from the country because of the war.

have
Students in Canada ~~has~~ studied a second language for many years.

REMEMBER: The verb must agree with the subject.

ACTIVITY 3 **Common Error 1.1**

Read each sentence. Underline the verb form that correctly completes each sentence.

1. Some nutritionists (*define* / *defines*) the United States as a "Fast Food Nation."

2. Research has shown that pollution and asthma (*is* / *are*) related.

3. Since 1990, environmentalists (*has developed* / *have developed*) amazing tools to improve recycling methods.

4. In this year's national report, the biggest increase in crime (*does not involve* / *do not involve*) violent physical crime but computer crime.

5. Social media companies (*has continued* / *have continued*) to experience significant growth.

6. In many western countries, the treatment of children with disabilities (*is not* / *are not*) different from the treatment of able-bodied children.

7. The new in-house exercise programs (*has benefited* / *have benefited*) both the employees of the company and the company itself.

8. Experts in business (*considers* / *consider*) honesty one of the most important qualities of a leader.

Common Error 1.2 Do you need simple present or present progressive?

tastes
Naan, a common Indian bread, ~~is tasting~~ delicious because it is cooked over a fire.

REMEMBER: Stative verbs are usually in the simple present.

Common Error 1.2

Read each sentence. Underline the verb form that correctly completes each sentence.

1. Private airline companies (*take / are taking*) the place of national airlines.

2. Recent research (*shows / is showing*) that trees belong to a type of social network.

3. People who are not comfortable with technology sometimes (*do not understand / are not understanding*) the instructions on software packages.

4. Tourists (*visit / are visiting*) Hong Kong in record numbers these days.

5. If an experiment sample size is too small, the size (*ruins / is ruining*) the results.

6. Environmental scientists are concerned because icebergs (*melt / are melting*) at a very fast rate.

7. Teachers report that the new art education program (*improves / is improving*) students' critical thinking skills.

8. According to some sociologists, pure democracy (*does not exist / is not existing*) in the world today.

Common Error 1.3 Do you need simple present or present perfect?

has increased
The number of biomedical engineers ~~increases~~ significantly since 2005.

REMEMBER: With the adverbs of time *for* or *since*, use the present perfect. Do not use the simple present.

ACTIVITY 5 **Common Error 1.3**

Fill in the blanks with the correct simple present or present perfect form of the verb in parentheses.

1. Economists _____ (*study*) the possibility
   of an upcoming depression for more than 10 years. In fact, many of them
   _____ (*believe*) that things will become worse
   before they become better.

2. Today, only 35,000 people in Canada _____ (*speak*)
   one of the Inuit languages. They have spoken these languages for centuries, but now
   the languages _____ (*be*) at risk.

3. Scientists say that tomatoes _____ (*qualify*) as fruits, not vegetables. Today, approximately 7,500 tomato varieties _____ (*exist*) around the world.

4. This radio station is vital because it _____ (*focus*) primarily on news reports. It _____ (*share*) information with millions of listeners in the United States.

5. Scientists _____ (*understand*) the significance of the environmental problem because they _____ (*study*) its effects for the past three decades.

6. Recent studies _____ (*show*) that eating too much red meat is unhealthy. Many doctors and dietitians _____ (*recommend*) eating between five and six ounces per day.

7. For over 30 years, the disaster of the space shuttle *Challenger* _____ (*remain*) in the consciousness of the American public. Most people _____ (*remember*) what they were doing at the time of the explosion in 1986.

8. According to the American Society for the Prevention of Cruelty to Animals, individuals _____ (*adopt*) almost 3 million shelter animals each year. While the number is high, many abandoned pets still _____ (*need*) a good home.

Academic Vocabulary

Verbs Frequently Used in Simple Present in Academic Writing

argue	change	define	increase	require
believe	come	illustrate	indicate	show

Source: Corpus of Contemporary American English (Davies 2008–)

ACTIVITY 6 **Vocabulary in Academic Writing**

Use the academic vocabulary in the simple present to complete each sentence. In some sentences, more than one answer is possible.

Subject Area	Example from Academic Writing
Economics	**1.** Economists often _____ about the cause of a stock market crash.
Paleontology	**2.** Recent findings _____ that giant alligators lived in North Africa thousands of years ago.
Criminal Justice	**3.** The statistics _____ a decrease in violent crime over the past few years.
Business	**4.** Many business experts _____ that low interest rates are very important for continued economic growth.
Literature	**5.** Robert Frost's language in "Directives" _____ symbolism perfectly.
Anthropology	**6.** Anthropologists _____ anthropology as the study of humanity.
Science / Engineering	**7.** Career opportunities in biomedical engineering _____ every year.
Science	**8.** The word "science" _____ from the Latin *scientia*, meaning knowledge.
Physics	**9.** Physics _____ a very strong understanding of mathematics, especially calculus.
Computer Science	**10.** Cloud computing, or online data storage, _____ the way people and computers interact.

Put It Together

Multiple Choice   Choose the letter of the correct answer.

1. Tataouine _____ a region of Tunisia where the original *Star Wars* was filmed.

   a. is   **b.** are   **c.** has been   **d.** are being

2. Because the number of people who die from cancer is increasing, doctors _____ to find the cure.

   a. race   **b.** races   **c.** is racing   **d.** are racing

3. Internships give students valuable work experience, but university students who have internships while they are studying _____ a lot of free time.

   a. does not have   **b.** do not have   **c.** is not having   **d.** are not having

4. Anthropologists who want to learn more about ancient man typically _____ to the frozen area of the Alps for their research.

   a. travels   **b.** travel   **c.** is traveling   **d.** are traveling

5. Psychologists these days _____ the connection between income level and happiness.

   a. research   **b.** researches   **c.** have researched   **d.** are researching

Error Correction   One of the five underlined words or phrases is not correct. Find the error and correct it. Be prepared to explain your answer.

6. According to film critics, there <u>are</u> several reasons why fans <u>love</u> the *Star Wars* films. One reason <u>is</u> the portrayal of the main characters. The other <u>has been</u> the conflict between the characters. Finally, <u>fans</u> are very happy with the actors.

7. The <u>idea</u> of the power of positive thinking <u>is</u> around for decades. Basically, positive thinking <u>involves</u> thinking good thoughts. Using positive thinking <u>leads</u> to pleasant feelings. These thoughts <u>help</u> both the psychological and physical self.

8. The Druze people <u>is</u> a religious group in the Middle East. Even though <u>their numbers</u> are <u>small</u>, their community <u>has banded</u> together for centuries. Although there <u>are</u> communities in other countries, most are in Lebanon.

The sun rises over the Arno River in Florence, Italy.

ACTIVITY 8   **Building Greater Sentences**

Combine these short sentences into one sentence. You can add new words and move words around, but you should not add or omit any ideas. More than one answer is possible, but these sentences require the simple present. (See Appendix 1, Building Greater Sentences, page 216, for tips on how to do this activity.)

1. **a.** Florence is a city.
   b. Florence is an Italian city.
   c. Florence is famous.
   d. It is the birthplace of the Renaissance.

   _____

   _____

2. **a.** The U.S. Constitution is a document.
   b. It is fairly long.
   c. It is easy to understand.

   _____

   _____

3. **a.** Music therapy is helpful.
   b. Music therapy helps people.
   c. These people have depression.
   d. Research has shown this.

   _____

   _____

Read the paragraph. Then follow the directions in the 10 steps to edit the information and composition of this paragraph. Write your revised paragraph on a separate sheet of paper. Be careful with capitalization and punctuation. Check your answers with the class.

DESCRIPTIVE PARAGRAPH

The Human Heart

¹The human heart is an amazing organ. ²It is responsible for pushing blood inside the circulatory system. ³The left side of the heart pumps blood to the entire body. ⁴The right side pumps blood to the lungs to receive oxygen. ⁵Our lungs do two things: they receive oxygen when we inhale and remove carbon dioxide when we exhale. ⁶Inside the lungs, the respiratory system interacts with the circulatory system. ⁷Then the blood moves to the right side of the heart into a filling chamber, which is called the right atrium. ⁸With each individual heartbeat, blood moves from the right atrium into a pumping chamber. ⁹After that, the blood picks up oxygen. ¹⁰Once the blood picks up oxygen, it pushes back to the heart, filling another chamber, which is called the left atrium. ¹¹Doctors want to expand their research into the blood circulation of the heart in order to have a better understanding of both the heart and the blood that pumps through our veins. ¹²The functions of the heart are truly amazing.

---

1. In sentence 1, change *an* to *probably the most.*

2. In sentence 2, change *it* to *this organ.*

3. In sentence 2, change the word *inside* to *throughout.*

4. Combine sentences 3 and 4 using *while*. Make any other necessary changes.

5. In sentence 5, change *our lungs* to *each lung.*

6. In sentence 6, change the *respiratory system* to *individuals' respiratory systems.*

7. In sentence 7, change *moves* to *flows*. We usually use this verb when referring to blood.

8. In sentence 10, the phrasal verb *picks up* is repetitive. Change *picks up* to *collects.*

9. Sentence 11 ends with the phrase *in order to have a better understanding of both the heart and the blood that pumps through our veins.* Move this phrase to the beginning of the sentence to improve sentence variety. Pay attention to punctuation.

10. In sentence 12, change the phrase *the functions of the heart* to *the way the heart functions.*

ACTIVITY 10 **Original Writing**

On a separate sheet of paper, write a descriptive paragraph (at least six sentences) about the characteristics of a particular person or thing. Use at least two examples of the simple present and one example of present perfect, and underline them.

Here are some examples of how to begin.

- *A good leader possesses three main characteristics.*
- *In order to be a successful student, one should do three things.*
- *A smart phone has several important functions.*

This statue of Marcus Aurelius, a Roman emperor during the *Pax Romana*, is in Rome, Italy.

2 Writing about the Past

WHAT DO YOU KNOW?

DISCUSS Look at the photo and read the caption. Discuss the questions.

1. What are the characteristics of a good leader? Are the characteristics the same today as in the past?

2. What was an important period in the history of your country? Why was it important?

FIND THE ERRORS This paragraph contains two errors with the past or past progressive. Find the errors and correct them. Explain your corrections to a partner.

DESCRIPTIVE PARAGRAPH

The *Pax Romana*

[1] The *Pax Romana*, Latin for Roman Peace, refers to a period of peace during the rule of the Roman Empire. [2] This period began in 31 BCE, when Augustus was defeating Marc Antony in a battle. [3] During this time, the Roman Empire was very strong, so citizens turn their attention from battles to engineering and the arts. [4] They focused on building roads and bridges, and it was during this time that they built the famous aqueducts. [5] The aqueducts were large structures that resembled bridges. [6] They carried water over long distances to supply fresh water to people who lived in the cities. [7] It was also during this time that the works of Roman poets, including Horace, Virgil, and Ovid, flourished and became popular. [8] The *Pax Romana*, an important period of peace and prosperity, lasted for about 200 years.

Grammar Forms

2.1 Simple Past

Subject	Verb	Example
I / you / he / she / it / we / they	verb + -ed (regular verb) irregular verb form	The period **ended** in 180 CE. The period **began** in 31 BCE.

Notes
1. In the simple past, regular verbs end in -ed. Add -ed (work – work**ed**), -d (arrive – arrive**d**), or change the y to i and add -ed (study – stud**ied**).
2. Irregular verbs in the past vary and do not end in -ed. Some common irregular verbs include go – went; have – had; and do – did.
3. See Appendix 4, Irregular Verbs, on page 220.

2.2 Past Form of *Be*

Subject	Verb	Example
I / he / she / it	*was* (irregular)	Lincoln **was** president during the American Civil War.
you / we / they	*were* (irregular)	The causes of the Civil War **were** complex.

2.3 Past Progressive

Subject	Verb	Example
I / he / she / it	*was* + verb + -*ing*	NASA **was monitoring** the space shuttle when it suddenly lost communication.
you / we / they	*were* + verb + -*ing*	The astronauts lost contact with NASA while they **were traveling** around the dark side of the moon.

2.4 Negative Past Forms

Form	Example
did not + verb	The essay **did not provide** supporting examples.
was / were + not	There **were not** many battles during that time.
was / were + not + verb + *-ing*	The product **was not selling** well in 2015.

Note
Contractions of negative forms are rare in academic writing.

ACTIVITY 1

Fill in the blank with the correct simple past form of the verb in parentheses. Use *not* when it is given.

1. A study by Manhattanville College _____ (*find*) that pet owners _____ (*be*) more satisfied with their lives.

2. On August 5, 1914, workers _____ (*install*) the first electric traffic signal in Cleveland, Ohio.

3. In the experiment, psychologists _____ (*ask*) participants to rate people's friendliness by the color of their clothing.

4. Alexis de Tocqueville, a French sociologist, _____ (*come*) to the United States in 1831. In 1835, he _____ (*write*) *Democracy in America*, a book about Americans' views on business, politics, and religion.

5. Because Steve Jobs and Steve Wozniak _____ (*not, have*) enough money to start Apple, they _____ (*sell*) some of their personal belongings in order to raise money.

6. While he _____ (*be*) in prison in the 1930s, the infamous Chicago criminal Al Capone _____ (*begin*) to suffer from dementia. He _____ (*die*) of cardiac arrest in Miami in 1947.

7. When the stock market prices _____ (*decrease*) in 2007, many investors panicked and _____ (*begin*) selling their stock.

8. In 2012, the U.S. men's soccer team _____ (*not, qualify*) for the Olympics.

Fill in the blank with the correct past progressive form of the verb given in parentheses. Use *not* when it is given.

1. While the main character of this story _____ (*conduct*) business in Italy, he had a small car accident that changed his life in an interesting way.

2. In the early 1800s, many American women who _____ (*work*) for women's rights did not get married because married women had fewer rights than single women.

3. The advertising company stated that it _____ (*not, try*) to mislead consumers with the claim its beauty cream would "eliminate wrinkles forever."

4. Henry Ford started an assembly line process because producing Ford Model T cars one at a time _____ (*take*) workers longer than he wanted.

5. A five-year study showed that dieters who _____ (*obtain*) most of their protein from fish and beans had lower cholesterol rates than those dieters who _____ (*eat*) beef and shellfish.

6. The independent investigation showed that many students in their first year of high school _____ (*lack*) basic mathematics and reading skills.

7. One reason the housing market _____ (*not, grow*) as fast as in previous years was an increase in interest rates.

8. Interviews with newly arrived immigrants showed they _____ (*have*) a difficult time adjusting to the new culture due to the language barrier.

Common Uses

2.5 Using Simple Past

The simple past is commonly used in writing to express an action completed in the past. It is used:

1. in narratives to report historical or past events	PAST NOW FUTURE The first televised presidential debate **occurred** in 1960 between John F. Kennedy and Richard Nixon.
2. to explain how an event occurred	After an unusually heavy rainfall, the river **overflowed** its banks and **flooded** the town.
3. in reports to describe methods or results of experiments	Seventy-five students **completed** a survey on their use of technology for assignments.
4. to introduce or cite another person's academic research	In her article, the author **stated** that current research on the topic is inadequate.

2.6 Using Past Progressive

The past progressive is used less commonly in writing. It expresses an action in progress in the past. It is used:

1. to show an action in progress that was interrupted by an action in the simple past	PILOT WAS LANDING TIRE BLEW OUT PAST NOW FUTURE One of the front tires blew out while the pilot **was landing** the plane.
2. to provide background information in a narrative	As President Kennedy stepped off the plane in Dallas, people **were cheering** and **clapping**.
3. to show an action in progress at a specific time in the past	At 10:30, the crowd **was gathering** outside the town hall.

Notes
1. Clauses in the past progressive often begin with *as, while,* or *when.*
2. With a series of verbs in the past progressive, it is not necessary to repeat *was* or *were.*
   Audience members **were taking** notes, **texting**, and **surfing** the Internet.

Fill in the blank with the correct simple past or past progressive form of the verb in parentheses. Use *not* when it is given. More than one answer may be possible.

1. Consumers continued to purchase the expensive new weight-loss product because it
_____ (*provide*) them with the fast and noticeable results they
_____ (*seek*).

2. The majority of immigrants who _____ (*come*) to the United States
after World War II _____ (*not make*) their decision to immigrate due
to political reasons, but rather due to economic ones.

3. The study found that a year after their arrival in the country, many of the immigrants
_____ (*attend*) English classes at school and
_____ (*develop*) their language skills.

4. Fifty years ago, academic counselors _____ (*advise*) young women
to pursue careers as teachers, nurses, and secretaries.

5. Studies by several notable university researchers showed that although some eastern cultures
_____ (*associate*) the color white with sadness or death, western
cultures often _____ (*have*) a positive association
with the color.

6. After applicants _____ (*take*) the Myers-Briggs Type Indicator test,
the Human Resource team interviewed those who _____ (*match*)
the company's business culture the best.

7. Compared to last year, Hollywood _____ (*not, produce*) many popular
comedies this year.

8. Last year's budget restrictions _____ (*not, allow*) the
technology department to purchase new computers even though many employees really
_____ (*need*) them.

Common Errors

Common Error 2.1   Is the simple past form correct?

explained
One group of scientists noted that global warming ~~did explain~~ the decrease in ice thickness in the Arctic.

In contrast, another group of scientists stated that fossil fuels such as coal and natural gas did not

contribute
~~contributed~~ to global warming.

REMEMBER: Use only one past form. Use the simple past form of the verb in affirmative sentences. Use *did* + *not* + the base form of the verb in negative sentences.

ACTIVITY 4   Common Error 2.1

There is one incorrect simple past verb form in each sentence or pair of sentences. Underline and correct the incorrect verb form.

1. According to U.S. census data from 1900, most people did not lived in large cities; by 1930, the opposite was true.

2. The medical team did identified the cause of the virus and began to research ways to eliminate it.

3. In the past, employers did often performed background checks on job applicants in order to confirm their previous work experience.

4. Data from the U.S. Department of Labor shows that from 1938 to 1968, the minimum wage did increased from 25 cents per hour to $1.60 per hour.

5. Many members of the so-called Traditionalist Generation, people who were born before 1946, did not viewed work as fun but rather as an obligation.

6. In the story, the main character looked and did see the bright blue sky through her open window; the window represented her future freedom.

7. In their study, psychologists did compared the grades of students who were procrastinators with those who were not.

8. Following a regular plan of exercise is not easy for many people. However, one study did showed that after only one month of exercising three times a week, people's fitness levels improved.

Common Error 2.2   Is the past progressive form correct?

living
He was ~~live~~ in Washington, D.C., when he decided to run for political office.

working
In the early 1960s, politicians were ~~worked~~ to pass civil rights legislation.

REMEMBER: Use *was / were* + verb + *-ing* with the past progressive.

ACTIVITY 5   **Common Error 2.2**

There is one incorrect past progressive verb form in each sentence. Underline and correct the error.

1. A majority of the young voters, those between the ages of 18 and 24, did not support the local candidate who was run for the office of state senator.

2. Malaysian Airlines Flight 370 was fly from Malaysia to China when it disappeared.

3. Only 31 percent of the citizens said the new insurance rules were work well.

4. When Czechoslovakia split into the Czech Republic and Slovakia in 1993, some people thought that the two countries were not do the correct thing.

5. In the 1997 car accident that killed Princess Diana, the driver was possibly drive more than 100 miles per hour.

6. The study focused on 86 Spanish speakers and 92 Arabic speakers who were attend an English language program in Orange County, California.

7. In the survey, citizens indicated that local traffic was become a problem for the community because of all the tourists who were visiting the area.

8. Because the cost of tuition was increase, many students decided to study part time.

Common Error 2.3   Do you need simple past or past progressive?

were crossing   sank
The soldiers ~~crossed~~ the Potomac in a storm when their boats ~~were sinking~~.

were waiting
At 6:30 a.m., hundreds of voters ~~waited~~ in line at the election polling stations.

saw
Upon their arrival in the colonies, the English settlers ~~were seeing~~ Native Americans for the first time.

REMEMBER: • Use simple past for a completed action or action that interrupts another action already in progress.
• Use past progressive for actions that were in progress at a specific time in the past.
• Nonaction verbs (verbs that describe a state) are usually not in the past progressive form.

In each paragraph, fill in the blanks with the correct form of the verbs in parentheses. More than one answer may be possible.

1.   During the early 1900s, jazz first _____ (*appear*) in New Orleans. From there, it _____ (*spread*) to other parts of the country. Soon musicians _____ (*play*) jazz music in clubs and _____ (*make*) records in Chicago, New York, and beyond.

2.   In 1889, a flood in Johnstown, Pennsylvania, _____ (*kill*) more than 2,000 people. Because of very heavy rain over several days, the South Fork dam above the town _____ (*break*), and water flowed quickly toward the town. People in Johnstown who _____ (*not, receive*) the news about the dangerous flooding or who _____ (*think*) there would be minimal flooding were lost in the powerful flood waters.

3.   Several factors _____ (*contribute*) to the formation of the Grand Canyon, one of which was water. When it _____ (*rain*), the soil was unable to absorb all of the water. As a result, the rain _____ (*flow*) down the Colorado River and _____ (*take*) soil and rocks with it. This often _____ (*cause*) powerful floods that _____ (*move*) huge rocks and boulders into the river. As the floods _____ (*push*) rocks and boulders down the river, the movement _____ (*eat*) away the land beside the river. This _____ (*allow*) the river to cut through the rock and _____ (*form*) the canyon.

4.   Large numbers of people _____ (*immigrate*) to the United States during the late nineteenth and early twentieth centuries. Many of them _____ (*seek*) economic opportunities, and others _____ (*look*) for religious freedom. During the early years of immigration, most migrants _____ (*come*) from Europe; later, the number of immigrants from Asia _____ (*increase*). Today, more people migrate to the United States from Asia and Latin America than from Europe.

Common Error 2.4   Are verb tenses consistent?

> was
> Barack Obama was elected president in 2008. He became president in January 2009, and he ~~is~~
> president for eight years.

REMEMBER: Do not change from one tense to another without a good reason.

ACTIVITY 7   **Common Error 2.4**

There is one incorrect verb form in each sentence or group of sentences. Underline and correct the incorrect verb form.

1. Joe Rantz, a 1936 Olympic gold medal winner, had a difficult childhood. His mother died when he was three. When Joe was 15, his father, stepmother, and their children move away and left him behind.

2. A recent survey of students pursuing degrees online showed that half of the students lived within 50 miles of the college. Students also said that cost is a major consideration when they chose online programs.

3. In 1776, the United States became a country with only 13 states. In 1791, Vermont joined the young country as the fourteenth state. A few months later, Kentucky enters the United States.

4. Schuyler Skaats Wheeler invented the fan in 1882. Philip Diehl, however, has the idea to attach a fan blade to a motor. He hung it from the ceiling and created the first ceiling fan.

5. In 1946, the Center for Disease Control concentrated on controlling the spread of diseases, but its mission changed later. For example, it works with the Food and Drug Administration to address food safety and nutrition issues after the Food Safety Modernization Act passed in 2011.

6. During the 1840s, pioneers in the United States traveled west in order to find work. They took all their possessions with them, and many just abandon their homes.

7. Jaguars were once plentiful in the United States, but an Arizona hunter shoot and killed the last female jaguar in 1963.

8. Health care has changed significantly over the years. In the past, patients remain in the hospital much longer, hospitals offered very little outpatient surgery, and doctors often gave patients minimal information about their condition.

Academic Vocabulary

Verbs Frequently Used in Past in the Academic Writing

be	begin	do	make	take
become	come	have	say	work

Source: Corpus of Contemporary American English (Davies 2008–)

ACTIVITY 8 **Vocabulary in Academic Writing**

Use the academic vocabulary in the simple past or past progressive to complete the sentences. Include *not* where given. For some sentences, more than one answer is possible.

Subject Area	Example from Academic Writing
Education	**1.** Many of the new teachers _____ (*not*) a degree in the subjects they were teaching.
Political Science	**2.** In the early 1930s, the number of workers who joined labor unions _____ to rise.
Environmental Science	**3.** The volunteers realized that by recycling, reusing, and reducing, they _____ a difference.
Psychology	**4.** It _____ the patient several years to overcome the effects of work-related stress.
History	**5.** Between 1933 and 1936, windstorms in part of the Great Plains blew much of the soil away, and the farmland _____ useless for growing crops.
Health	**6.** Before becoming the first female African-American general in the U.S. Army in 1979, Hazel Johnson-Brown _____ as chief of the Army Nurse Corps.
Economics	**7.** The financial advisors _____ (*not*) truthful about the risks involved in investing in growth stocks.
Business	**8.** Small, local businesses _____ well until the big chain stores started offering the same products for lower prices.
Computer Science	**9.** The field of computer science _____ from the need to calculate large amounts of data.
English Literature	**10.** One reviewer _____ that while the author's latest novel was enjoyable to read, it was not great literature.

Put It Together

Review Quiz

Multiple Choice   Choose the letter of the correct answer.

1. Leonardo Da Vinci both recorded his ideas and _____ pictures of them in a notebook.

   a. was drawing   **b.** drew   **c.** was drew   **d.** did draw

2. The National Defense Act of 1935 _____ the construction of six new air bases in the United States.

   a. was authorized   **b.** was authorizing   **c.** did authorize   **d.** authorized

3. On May 7, 1915, as the ocean liner *Lusitania* _____ near the coast of Ireland, a German U-boat sank the ship with torpedoes.

   a. was sailing   **b.** sailing   **c.** did sail   **d.** was sailed

4. In 1975, the results of a four-year study _____ that the subjects who reduced their salt consumption lowered their blood pressure by more than 6 percent.

   a. were showing   **b.** showed   **c.** was showing   **d.** was showed

5. Cellist Yo-Yo Ma, who was born in France to Chinese parents, _____ in the United States.

   a. was grown up   **b.** was growing up   **c.** grew up   **d.** did grew up

Error Correction   One of the five underlined words or phrases is not correct. Find the error and correct it. Be prepared to explain your answer.

6. Frida Kahlo, <u>who</u> is well-known for her many self-portraits, first <u>began</u> to paint while she <u>was recovering</u> after a bus accident <u>was making</u> her unable to walk <u>for three months</u>.

7. When architects first <u>developed</u> "green" buildings, many of them <u>were having</u> energy-saving features. In order to <u>conserve</u> water, architects also <u>designed</u> landscapes with plants that <u>were</u> native to the area.

8. In the 1920s, as car <u>ownership</u> in the United States <u>increased</u> and people <u>traveled</u> farther from home, many other changes <u>such as</u> paved roads, traffic signals, and gas stations also <u>occur</u>.

There are an estimated 100 to 180 panthers in the wild in Florida.

Building Greater Sentences

Combine these short sentences into one sentence. You can add new words and move words around, but you should not add or omit any ideas. More than one answer is possible, but these sentences require past verb forms. (See Appendix 1, Building Greater Sentences, page 216, for tips on how to do this activity.)

1. a. Florida biologists put a collar on an endangered male panther.
 b. This occurred in early 1986.
 c. The biologists monitored the panther for almost nine years.
 d. The panther died in 1994.

_____

_____

2. a. A marine biologist was looking for whales.   **c.** She spotted a group of dolphins.
 b. This was off the Washington coast.   **d.** The dolphins were rare.

_____

_____

3. a. The *Titanic* sailed from England to the United States.
 b. This was in 1912.
 c. The *Titanic* hit an iceberg.
 d. The iceberg was huge.
 e. The *Titanic* sank.

_____

_____

Read the paragraph. Then follow the directions in the 10 steps to edit the information and composition of this paragraph. Write your revised paragraph on a separate piece of paper. Be careful with capitalization and punctuation. Check your answers with the class.

NARRATIVE PARAGRAPH

The Beginning of World War I

[1] June 28, 1914, was a huge date in history. [2] Archduke Ferdinand of Austria-Hungary was visiting Sarajevo, which is in Bosnia-Herzogovina. [3] The Archduke was riding through the city in an open car. [4] A teenager shot the Archduke. [5] He killed the Archduke, and he also killed the Archduke's wife. [6] This event caused a series of actions that resulted in the start of World War I. [7] Austria-Hungary declared war on Serbia. [8] A week later, Germany, Russia, and France were involved. [9] Belgium, Montenegro, and Great Britain were also involved. [10] This war lasted four years and resulted in the deaths of millions of people. [11] Most people have heard about this war. [12] Very few actually know how the war began.

1. In sentence 1, the word *huge* sounds informal and conversational. Change *huge* to the more formal academic adjective *important*.

2. In sentence 1, add the word *extremely* in the correct place and change *history* to *the history of the world*.

3. Begin sentence 2 with the transition *on that date* and add the correct punctuation.

4. The Archduke was with his wife. Add *with his wife* before *in an open car* in sentence 3.

5. The teenager also shot the Archduke's wife. Add *and the Archduke's wife* to sentence 4.

6. Combine sentences 3 and 4. Begin the new sentence with *While* and add the correct punctuation.

7. Sentence 5 is wordy. Rewrite it so that it has only one subject and one verb.

8. In sentence 6, add the adjective *single* before event and the adjective *political* before *actions*.

9. There is no transition between sentences 6 and 7. Begin sentence 7 with the prepositional phrase *on July 28* and add the correct punctuation.

10. Combine sentences 8 and 9 into one sentence. Then combine sentences 11 and 12 into one sentence using the word *although*.

Original Writing

On a separate sheet of paper, write a narrative paragraph (at least six sentences) about an important or well-known historical event or cultural aspect of your country. Use at least two examples of past verbs and underline them; try to use more if possible.

Here are some examples of how to begin.

- *On August 5, 2010, the entire world watched the rescue of the men trapped in Chile's San José mine.*
- *All of Cuba cheered when two of its boxers, Robeisy Ramirez and Roniel Iglesias won Olympic gold medals in 2012.*
- *The Japanese art of origami began in the 6th century and, over the years, spread to countries throughout the world.*

Measuring sticks for the water level no longer serve their purpose at the Diglab Dam in Jordan. After years of drought, the reservoir has shrunk.

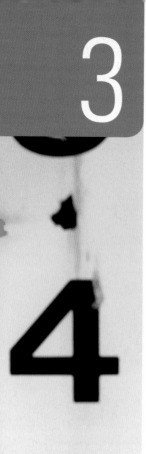

3 Writing with the Present Perfect

WHAT DO YOU KNOW?

DISCUSS Look at the photo and read the caption. Discuss the questions.

1. Does your country have a drought problem? If so, how long has it been a problem?

2. Have you noticed any signs of global warming? If so, what are they?

FIND THE ERRORS This paragraph contains two errors with the present perfect. Find the errors and correct them. Explain your corrections to a partner.

> INTRODUCTORY PARAGRAPH

Global Warming

[1] According to scientists who study global warming, the temperature of the earth is rising, and it is humans who are causing this situation. [2] In the last century, the temperature of the planet has risen on average 1.53 degrees Fahrenheit. [3] For the past two decades, people debated this issue. [4] Some people still refuse to believe that global warming exists. [5] Others accept that it exists and that it is an urgent problem, but they do not agree on its causes or on the solutions. [6] The fact is that the planet has become warmer, and understanding the causes of global warming will help us to solve this problem. [7] This paper will examine three ways in which human beings have contribute to global warming.

Grammar Forms

3.1 Present Perfect

Subject	Verb	Example
I / you / we / they	*have* + (*not*) + past participle	Scientists **have studied** global warming for years. World leaders **have not done** enough to stop global warming.
he / she / it	*has* + (*not*) + past participle	The university **has conducted** an annual survey of transfer students since 1984. The new leader **has not been** in power for very long.

Notes
1. For regular verbs, the past participle is the same as the simple past: verb + -ed. For example, *work–worked; arrive–arrived; study–studied*.
2. See Appendix 4, Irregular Verbs, on page 220 for a list of irregular past participles.

ACTIVITY 1

Fill in the blank with the correct present perfect form of the verb in parentheses. Use *not* when it is given.

1. This research paper will discuss why scholars _____ (*write*) so passionately about this issue.

2. According to historians, plastic surgery _____ (*exist*) since 600 BCE.

3. For a variety of reasons, the field of cultural anthropology _____ (*not, increase*) in popularity.

4. The capital of Canada _____ (*be*) Ottawa since 1867.

5. Surprisingly, doctors _____ (*not, find*) a cure for the common cold yet.

6. Of the more than 300 Americans who _____ (*win*) the Nobel Prize, approximately 30 percent were born outside of the United States.

7. Latin _____ (*become*) a "dead" language, at least in its spoken form.

8. Since 1918, women in the United Kingdom _____ (*have*) the right to vote.

Common Uses

3.2 Using Present Perfect

The present perfect is very common in writing. It is used:

1. to express an important change that has occurred at an indefinite time in the past (when it happened is not important) • This is common in the introduction of a paragraph or essay, often with the adverb *recently*.	 PAST NOW FUTURE Only twelve people **have walked** on the moon. Many people **have** recently **criticized** the new driver's license requirements.
2. to indicate that an action has not happened but may soon happen (with *not . . . yet*)	Researchers **have** not **discovered** a cure for cancer yet.
3. to refer to a situation that began in the past and continues to the present • This use often occurs with the phrases *since* + point in time and *for* + length of time.	 1960 PAST NOW FUTURE Brasilia **has been** the capital of Brazil since 1960. Public officials **have known** about this problem for decades.
4. to refer to an action that has happened several times in the past (no specific past time) and may happen again • This commonly occurs with the phrase (*number of*) *times*.	Humans **have landed** on the moon about 15 times.
5. to indicate that a person or thing has or has not had the experience of doing something (*indefinite past*)	This area **has** never **experienced** an earthquake.

Note

The question form is commonly used with the adverb *ever*. It is sometimes used as the opening hook for a paragraph or essay.

    Have you ever **experienced** a natural disaster?

Fill in the blank with the correct present perfect form of the verb in parentheses. Use *not* when it is given. Be ready to explain why the present perfect is used.

1. Tonight's lecture will explain why many children _____ (*become*) obese.

2. Since its independence in 2011, South Sudan _____ (*face*) a number of both national and international difficulties.

3. The health professionals in that program _____ (*not, persuade*) many patients to eat better or exercise more.

4. This law _____ (*do*) very little to reduce crime.

5. In recent economic reports, some leaders _____ (*suggest*) that interest rates will rise.

6. Scientists do not know what _____ (*cause*) the recent decrease in the honeybee population.

7. The province of Quebec _____ (*vote*) twice on whether to separate from Canada to become an independent country.

8. There are several reasons why the economy _____ (*not, grow*) over the past five years.

9. Michael Phelps _____ (*win*) more gold medals than any other Olympic athlete.

10. Chocolate arrived in Europe around 1550, so Europeans _____ (*know*) about chocolate for almost 500 years.

Common Errors

Common Error 3.1 Do you need simple present or present perfect?

has been
Brasilia ~~is~~ the capital of Brazil since 1960.

REMEMBER: If the action began in the past and is still true, use the present perfect. Do not use the simple present.

ACTIVITY 3 Common Error 3.1

Underline the correct verb.

1. The stock market (*is / has been*) strong since the beginning of the month.

2. The earth (*revolves / has revolved*) around the sun.

3. Wimbledon (*is / has been*) the oldest tennis tournament in the world.

4. These special clocks (*have / have had*) displays that the blind can read by using the sense of touch.

5. Monarchs (*rule / have ruled*) Thailand for over 800 years.

6. Due to the short growing season this year, farms in the region (*produce / have produced*) smaller crops than usual.

7. Canada (*has / has had*) two official languages, English and French, since the Official Languages Act came into effect on September 11, 1972.

8. Humans (*do not sneeze / have not sneezed*) when sleeping because the reflex that causes a sneeze cannot send signals to the brain when a person is asleep.

Common Error 3.2 Do you need simple past or present perfect?

announced
At the annual company meeting yesterday, the bank president ~~has announced~~ that the downtown office will close next month.

have come
Five United States presidents ~~came~~ from the state of Virginia.

REMEMBER: • Use simple past with specific past times such as *yesterday*, *last month*, and *one year ago*.
• Use present perfect with actions that may happen again in the future.

Fill in the blanks with the correct simple past or present perfect form of the verbs in parentheses.

1. Throughout history, people _____ (use) elephants in art and popular culture. For example, an elephant _____ (appear) on a U.S. postage stamp in 2014.

2. For more than seven decades, Air France _____ (be) the largest airline in France. In 1946, this company _____ (begin) flying from Paris to New York. Since then, millions of passengers _____ (fly) on this airline.

3. Everyone _____ (hear) about the Olympics, but what do people really know about this event? The modern Olympics _____ (begin) a little over a century ago. In 1896, only 241 athletes from 14 nations _____ (participate) in the Olympic Games, but participation in this world event _____ (grow) to more than 10,000 athletes from more than 200 countries.

4. In 1981, Prince Charles _____ (marry) Diana Spencer, who most of us remember as Princess Diana. An international television audience of 750 million people _____ (watch) this event, which _____ (be) a record number at the time.

5. Russia was the largest country within the former Soviet Union, which _____ (become) a country in 1922 and _____ (exist) until 1991.

6. World War II _____ (end) in 1944. However, some countries still _____ (not, recover) from its after effects.

7. Christopher Columbus _____ (navigate) to the Americas in 1492. He _____ (return) to Spain in 1493.

Academic Vocabulary

Verbs Frequently Used in Present Perfect in Academic Writing

be	come	give	make	show
become	do	have	see	take

Source: Biber, D., et al. (1999). *Longman Grammar of Spoken and Written English.* New York: Longman.

ACTIVITY 5   **Vocabulary in Academic Writing**

Use the academic vocabulary in the present perfect to complete the sentences.

Subject Area	Example from Academic Writing
Education	**1.** The technology and engineering educators _____ many steps to improve the education they provide students.
Political Science	**2.** Despite international objections, dictators have recently risen to power in several major countries. Four factors _____ these leaders an advantage: modern communications, new military technology, government support, and a lack of outside inquiry.
Environmental Science	**3.** The Industrial Revolution _____ underway for about two centuries.
Technical Writing	**4.** Government agencies typically do not fund the projects that grant applicants _____ but rather the projects that they plan to do.
History	**5.** In the last decade, historians _____ an increase in the public's interest in colonial photographs.
Health	**6.** Studies _____ that people with lower birth weights experience increased rates of heart disease.
Economics	**7.** Population shifts, greater world trade, unemployment, and the advance of technology all _____ an effect on today's job market.
English Composition	**8.** Although soccer _____ an important part of the American sports scene, it will never replace football, basketball, and baseball in the hearts of American sports fans.
Computer Science	**9.** The use of specialized techniques in the design of computer experiments has progressed remarkably in the past two decades, but how far _____ this technology _____?
Asian Studies	**10.** The agriculture industry in Vietnam _____ great progress, resulting in less poverty, better nourishment, and increased food exports.

Put It Together

Review Quiz

Multiple Choice   Choose the letter of the correct answer.

1. Wolfgang Amadeus Mozart, who was a famous Austrian composer, _____ born in 1756.

   a. is   **b.** was   **c.** has been   **d.** have been

2. The Euro _____ as the currency of most European countries since 1999.

   a. exists   **b.** exist   **c.** existed   **d.** has existed

3. Tech stocks have recently _____ tremendously, but many analysts say these stocks have even more potential for investment growth.

   a. rose   **b.** risen   **c.** rise   **d.** rising

4. Last month our state experienced record cold temperatures, but now the warm weather _____, allowing local residents to enjoy the outdoors again.

   a. returned   **b.** has returned   **c.** was returning   **d.** returns

5. Over the past decade, the number of biotech companies in San Francisco _____ dramatically.

   a. has increased   **b.** increased   **c.** was increasing   **d.** have increased

Error Correction   One of the five underlined words or phrases is not correct. Find the error and correct it. Be prepared to explain your answer.

6. Many people have recently criticize Congress because less than a month ago it

   raised taxes by almost five percent.

7. Due to external pressure, several clothing companies have decided to cancel their

   business relationship with factories at countries with poor working conditions.

8. Telephone usage is changing, and cell phones are replacing land lines all over the

   world. In Argentina, for example, 2010 statistics have revealed that there were over

   31 million cell phone users.

A castle rises out of the ruins of the ancient city of Al-Ula, Saudi Arabia.

Building Greater Sentences

Combine these short sentences into one sentence. You can add new words and move words around, but you should not add or omit any ideas. More than one answer is possible, but these sentences require present perfect. (See Appendix 1, Building Greater Sentences, page 216, for tips on how to do this activity.)

1. a. Al-Ula is an ancient city.
   b. It is in Saudi Arabia.
   c. The last residents left in 1983.
   d. It has not been occupied since that time.

_____

_____

2. a. Singapore and Malaysia used to be one country.
   b. Singapore is independent.
   c. This separation took place in 1965.

_____

_____

3. a. China is a country.
   b. It is very big.
   c. China has only one time zone.
   d. This has been true since 1949.

_____

_____

Steps to Composing

Read the paragraph. Then follow the directions in the 10 steps to edit the information and composition of this paragraph. Write your revised paragraph on a separate sheet of paper. Be careful with capitalization and punctuation. Check your answers with the class.

CAUSE-EFFECT PARAGRAPH

Murray College

[1] Last year, Murray College helped 5,000 students graduate. [2] The majority of them got jobs almost immediately. [3] A good number of these students entered graduate programs. [4] Therefore, it is not surprising that Murray College is frequently ranked as one of the best colleges. [5] Why does Murray College have this high ranking? [6] First of all, students and their parents are very satisfied with Murray College's high job placement rate. [7] The second reason involves money. [8] Despite the rising cost of everything last year, tuition at Murray remained relatively low. [9] Finally, students appreciate the small classes with professors who take a strong interest in student success. [10] Last year, graduates from Murray College said that the college was an excellent investment in their future.

1. In sentence 1, change *last year* to *since opening its doors in 1990*. Change the verb if needed.

2. In sentence 1, change *5,000* to *more than 10,000*.

3. In sentence 2, change the informal phrase *got jobs* to *entered the workforce*.

4. Connect sentences 2 and 3. Begin the new sentence with *while*.

5. In sentence 4, add the prepositional phrase *in the country* in the best location.

6. In sentence 5, change *have this high ranking* to *rank so high*.

7. The adjective *high* is repeated in sentences 5 and 6. In sentence 6, change *high* to *excellent*.

8. In sentence 8, change *last year* to *today*. Then change the verb to match the new adverb of time.

9. In sentence 9 add the adjective *helpful* to describe *professors*.

10. In sentence 10, change *last year* to *since it opened over a decade ago*. Change the verb if needed.

ACTIVITY 9 **Original Writing**

On a separate sheet of paper, write a cause-effect paragraph (at least six sentences) about a current issue or situation. Use at least two examples of the present perfect and underline them; try to use three if possible.

Here are some examples of how to begin.

- *The use of drones by private citizens has rapidly increased in recent years.*
- *Andy Garcia has changed the way that many people view Cuban-American actors.*
- *Reality TV shows have changed a great deal since they were first introduced.*

College students participate in a climbing competition.

4 Writing about the Future

WHAT DO YOU KNOW?

DISCUSS Look at the photo and read the caption. Discuss the questions.

1. What kinds of resources and services do most colleges have for students? Why are they important for students?

2. Why are recreational facilities important for college students?

FIND THE ERRORS This paragraph contains two errors with verbs in the future. Find the errors and correct them. Explain your corrections to a partner.

INTRODUCTORY PARAGRAPH

Ethnography Proposal

[1] This ethnographic case study will focus on a group of five first-year college students. [2] The group will include both students who have chosen a major and those who have not. [3] The study will to seek to identify the types of campus resources available to these students and how often the students use them. [4] Campus resources may include both academic and nonacademic ones. [5] Academic resources might include the library and its tutoring services. [6] Nonacademic resources might consist of access to exercise equipment and on-campus movies. [7] The study takes place during the upcoming fall semester and will last approximately eight weeks. [8] Data collection methods will include both observations of participants and follow-up interviews. [9] Notes from interviews will be transcribed and analyzed in order to categorize the types of resources that are used and the frequency of their use.

Grammar Forms

4.1 Future with *Will*

Subject	Verb	Example
I / you / he / she it / we / they	*will* + verb	This paper **will explore** the economic effects of the American Civil War.
I / you / he / she it / we / they	*will* + *not* + verb	Because of manufacturing problems, the company **will not meet** the next quarter's demand for its products.

Note
Contractions are almost never used in academic writing.

4.2 Future with *Be Going To*

Subject	Verb	Example
I he / she / it you / we / they	*am going to* + verb *is going to* + verb *are going to* + verb	Over a six-week period, participants in the medical study **are going to record** the number of calories that they consume.
I he / she / it you / we / they	*am not going to* + verb *is not going to* + verb *are not going to* + verb	The new tax law **is not going to affect** people who earn less than $65,000 annually.

4.3 Future with *May*

Subject	Verb	Example
I / you / he / she it / we / they	*may* + verb	For now, polar bears still roam the Arctic Circle, but that **may change** as sea ice continues to melt.
I / you / he / she it / we / they	*may* + *not* + verb	The Supreme Court **may not make** a decision about labor union fees for another month.

4.4 Other Expressions of Future Time

For future time clauses, use the simple present in the time clause, and use the future in the independent clause.	When the heavy rains **come**, the reservoirs **will fill** again.
In a real conditional sentence, use the simple present in the *if* clause, and use *will* or *may* in the independent clause.	If the government **invests** in this research, doctors **may find** a cure more quickly.

ACTIVITY 1

Read the following sentences. Underline the future form of the verb in each sentence. If the verb form is correct, write C on the line in front of the sentence. If the verb is incorrect, write X on the line. Then write the correct word(s) above the sentence.

_____ **1.** Crime will continue to increase until communities form neighborhood watch groups.

_____ **2.** Over the next 10 years, educational researchers are going to study the effects of technology on the way children learn.

_____ **3.** Consumers are more comfortable shopping online when they know the companies will not to make personal information available to other businesses.

_____ **4.** Future studies of natural remedies for anxiety may provide the answers that doctors and their patients are seeking.

_____ **5.** After-school programs provide the structure and environment many students need so they will not become victims of violent crime.

_____ **6.** Although many Alzheimers patients lose the ability to speak, art therapy may to help them communicate.

_____ **7.** It is likely that people who plan ahead for a hurricane are going to survive.

_____ **8.** Reducing financial aid for students in need will to force many of them to leave college.

Common Uses

In academic writing, *will* is used:

1. to make a prediction about the future, usually one of strong certainty • Predictions are often in concluding statements.	Unless the government makes changes, the Great Lakes **will not recover** from their current state of pollution. This species **will likely become** extinct within the next 30 years.
2. to introduce or state the plan or purpose of a paper	This paper **will explore** the economic effects of the Civil War on the South.
3. to add ideas for future work or research	Future research **will focus** on how to implement this new technology.
4. to express a future possibility in a real conditional sentence	If Congress passes the new minimum wage law, many workers **will get** significant raises.

Notes
1. Certain adverbs can strengthen or weaken predictions with *will*: *likely, probably, possibly, definitely,* and *certainly.*
2. Other common verbs that introduce the purpose of a paper include *examine, discuss, analyze,* and *report.*

4.6 | Using *May*

May is sometimes used in academic writing to express future possibilities. It is used:

1. to make a prediction about the future, usually one of weak certainty • Predictions are often in concluding statements.	New medicines **may eliminate** these global health issues. When the new tax law is passed, workers **may be able to save** more money for retirement.
2. to state a future possibility	In the near future, researchers **may find** new solutions for these global health issues.

Be going to is more common in spoken English than in academic writing.

Use *be going to* to make a prediction about the future, usually one made with certainty.	Researchers **are going to analyze** the data to look for response patterns.

ACTIVITY 2

For each sentence, underline the future form of the verb. Then write the letter of the reason for using the future verb form from the box.

a. make a strong prediction	**c.** state a future condition
b. state a plan	**d.** make a weak prediction

_____ **1.** Today's obese children will pay for their disease by experiencing serious illness and high medical costs in the future.

_____ **2.** As part of the study, researchers are going to take water samples from three nearby lakes twice a week for six months.

_____ **3.** Additional research may provide scientists with more effective tests for determining who is at risk of developing this life-threatening illness.

_____ **4.** In our future global economy, being bilingual will definitely give job applicants an advantage when looking for a job.

_____ **5.** If the Board of Education collects data from all the schools, the information will help identify what to change in the curriculum.

_____ **6.** Due to rising labor costs overseas, many computer and electronics manufacturers may need to move their businesses back to the United States.

_____ **7.** Social media will become even more valuable if companies use it to obtain consumers' opinions about every product they use.

_____ **8.** The study will require participants to answer survey questions about their daily computer use.

Common Errors

Common Error 4.1   Is the correct verb form used after *will* or *may*?

benefit

Studies have shown that regular meditation will ~~to benefit~~ people both physically and mentally.

REMEMBER: Use the base form of the verb after *will* or *may*, not the infinitive (*to* + verb) form. Do not add an *-s, -ed,* or *-ing* ending.

ACTIVITY 3   **Common Error 4.1**

Read each sentence. Underline the correct verb form in parentheses.

1. This paper (*will to describe / will describe*) two ways employers use social media to hire workers and (*will evaluates / will evaluate*) each use.

2. Researchers hope that they (*will finding / will find*) the causes of schizophrenia and that this discovery (*may helping / may help*) prevent the disorder.

3. Limiting the time children use electronic devices (*will likely result / will likely results*) in their developing better social skills.

4. Power companies that charge customers too much (*may to be / may be*) responsible for repaying them tens of millions of dollars.

5. Higher fees (*may to lead / may lead*) many senior citizens to decide against reverse mortgages.

6. Although the results of this health and fitness study are not conclusive, they (*will guiding / will guide*) future research.

7. Additional data from wildlife managers (*may confirm / may confirms*) that wolves and bears indeed caused the decline in the elk population in the nation's wilderness parks.

8. In order to begin solving their clean-water problems, some countries (*may needing / may need*) to supply their citizens with water filters and build water tanks to collect and filter rain.

Common Error 4.2   Do you need to use *will* or *may*?

will require

This experiment ~~may require~~ participants to record their daily exercise over the next three months.

may show

Further studies ~~will show~~ which types of exercise provide the greatest health benefits.

REMEMBER: Use *will* to express strong certainty and *may* to express less certainty or possibility.

In each sentence, fill in the blank with *will* or *may* and the verb in parentheses. Use *not* and an adverb of certainty when it is given. Consider the writer's degree of certainty in each sentence when choosing your answer.

1. It is likely that, based on the ease and convenience of streaming music, the industry _____ (*face*) increased competition from new services, which _____ (*definitely benefit*) the listeners.

2. Despite the fact that online education is convenient and sometimes even less expensive than many face-to-face courses, the traditional university _____ (*not, disappear*) in the near future.

3. Using the social media strategies outlined in this marketing proposal _____ (*save*) the company both time and money and also _____ (*increase*) company revenues.

4. Researchers found that having a support system when one is young _____ (*help*) one handle the stress that occurs in everyday life later on.

5. According to recent research, companies that include employees in the decision-making process _____ (*find*) increased motivation among workers, which _____ (*lead*) to higher company profits.

6. It is clear that even after the county agricultural department implements the proposed solution, residents _____ (*not, benefit*) from the pesticide ban for at least a decade.

7. The anthropological team announced that artifacts at the excavation site _____ (*mean*) that a community of indigenous people lived in the area over 150,000 years ago. Continued digging _____ (*confirm*) their theory.

8. Despite the company's statement that it _____ (*stop*) illegal dumping of hazardous waste immediately, environmental clean-up crews believe that the environment _____ (*not, recover*) from the damage that has been done.

Common Error 4.3   Does the clause need a future or present verb?

> *become*
> Most immigrants will adapt to a new culture after they ~~will become~~ familiar with the customs.
>
> *are*
> If the results ~~will be~~ unsatisfactory, they will need to redesign the experiment.

REMEMBER: • Use the future in the independent clause and simple present in the dependent clause (the time clause).
          • For real conditional sentences, use the simple present in the dependent clause (the *if* clause) and the future in the independent clause.

ACTIVITY 5   **Common Error 4.3**

Read the following paragraphs. Find the complex sentences. Underline the six verb errors in the main and dependent clauses. Then write the correction above each error.

Effective Study Techniques

¹ Researchers at a local university are planning a study to identify effective study techniques. ² One technique they will explore is self-testing. ³ Results from previous studies show that if students will test themselves before taking an exam, they will do better on the exam.

⁴ Researchers believe that successful learners use other strategies, and the study will identify those strategies. ⁵ Before the researchers choose the participants, the volunteers will complete a survey about their study habits. ⁶ The researchers will then select volunteers for the study. ⁷ The experiment will begin as soon as there will be 50 volunteers. ⁸ When the students will work in their assigned groups, they will keep logs of their study habits, test scores, and end-of-term grades.

⁹ After researchers collect and analyze the data, they will make specific recommendations. ¹⁰ If the study results are significant, the university will provide strategy training for its professors. ¹¹ Researchers believe students become better learners if teachers will use these strategies in their classrooms. ¹² If researchers are able to identify additional strategies that successful students use, they will also implement workshops for students. ¹³ However, researchers will not recommend any curriculum changes unless the results of the study will be significant.

Academic Vocabulary

Verbs Frequently Used in the Future in Academic Writing

be	come	go	have	lead
become	do	happen	know	need

Source: Corpus of Contemporary American English (Davies 2008–)

ACTIVITY 6 **Vocabulary in Academic Writing**

Use the academic vocabulary in the future with *will*, *be going to*, or *may* to complete the sentences. More than one answer may be possible.

Subject Area	Example from Academic Writing
Education	**1.** Across the nation, teacher shortages _____ a critical issue as fewer people seek careers in teaching.
Political Science	**2.** More than half of the survey respondents think reducing global warming _____ to more government regulation.
Environmental Science	**3.** A coal mine fire in Pennsylvania began in 1962, and officials believe it _____ on burning for 200 years or more.
Psychology	**4.** A team of psychologists has compiled 20 statements for respondents to rate so they _____ if what they are feeling is love.
History	**5.** The changes that _____ when a country's new leader takes power are difficult to predict.
Health	**6.** The physical therapist _____ the exercises with the patient to make sure the patient understands how to do them.
Economics	**7.** For now, the trade section of the Central America Association Agreement _____ in effect.
Business	**8.** A recent market analysis predicts that during the holidays, tourists _____ to the new area for shopping and entertainment.
Computer Science	**9.** The Bureau of Labor Statistics projects that, over the next 10 years, the country _____ close to 90,000 computer support specialists.
English	**10.** Students who take literature courses _____ better communication skills and a deeper understanding of other cultures.

Put It Together

ACTIVITY 7 **Review Quiz**

Multiple Choice   Choose the letter of the correct answer.

1. The purpose of this research project is to identify specific careers that offer job satisfaction and _____ in demand for the next decade.

   a. will be   **b.** will to be   **c.** will not be   **d.** will being

2. As people in their late fifties and early sixties begin planning for their retirement, many _____ moving to a smaller home in an effort to reduce costs.

   a. may to consider   **b.** may considered   **c.** may consider   **d.** going to consider

3. For many people, volunteering is a positive activity because they believe that they _____ a difference in another person's life.

   a. going to make   **b.** will going to make   **c.** are going to make   **d.** will to make

4. If the president does not sign or veto a bill within 10 days after he receives it, and Congress is still in session, the bill _____ law.

   a. will becoming   **b.** will became   **c.** become   **d.** will become

5. Nutritionists recommend drinking green tea because its powerful antioxidant properties _____ one's risk of cancer.

   a. are gonna lower   **b.** may lower   **c.** will lowers   **d.** may to lower

Error Correction   One of the five underlined words or phrases is not correct. Find the error and correct it. Be prepared to explain your answer.

6. After examining all of the data, school officials strongly <u>believe</u> that a longer school year <u>will helping</u> students to <u>remember</u> more and <u>forget</u> less <u>during</u> the summer break.

7. The Ocean Cleanup Project predicts that it <u>may to be</u> possible over the next 10 years <u>to remove</u> almost half of the plastic that <u>is floating</u> in the Pacific Ocean and <u>to sell</u> it to companies that <u>will recycle</u> it.

8. When companies <u>use</u> artificial intelligence <u>to do</u> work instead of <u>using</u> humans, the unemployment rate <u>is increasing</u> significantly, and poverty rates <u>may rise</u> as well.

An inventor controls a snake robot in a lab at Carnegie Mellon University in Pittsburgh, Pennsylvania.

Building Greater Sentences

Combine these short sentences into one sentence. You can add new words and move words around, but you should not add or omit any ideas. More than one answer is possible, but all of these sentences require future forms.

1. a. Robots are going to replace human workers.
   b. Robots are more efficient than human workers.
   c. Robots also cost less than human workers.
   d. Some economists fear this.

---

2. a. It is possible that businesses will lose customers.
   b. It is possible that businesses will lose sales.
   c. Studies show this.
   d. These businesses are new.
   e. This happens when the businesses display too little merchandise.

---

3. a. People will die in traffic accidents this year.
   b. This year's number will be higher than last year's number.
   c. This year's number is approximately 8 percent higher.
   d. The National Highway Safety Administration predicts this.

Read the paragraph from a psychology project proposal. Then follow the directions in the 10 steps to edit the information and composition of this paragraph. Write your revised paragraph on a separate piece of paper. Be careful with capitalization and punctuation. Check your answers with the class.

PROCESS PARAGRAPH

Project Proposal

[1] For this psychology project, I will copy the change blindness experiment from chapter 7 in our textbook. [2] The change blindness experiment tests how well people notice changes that happen. [3] For this experiment, I will stand behind the checkout desk in the library and hand out a short library survey and a pencil to students when they check out books. [4] I will hand them the pencil. [5] I will accidentally drop the pencil. [6] When I bend down to get the pencil, my partner, who is down behind the desk out of sight, will stand up and give the pencil to the student while I stay down and out of sight. [7] We will record whether the student noticed the change and whether the student said anything. [8] The differences between us are going to be very obvious. [9] My partner does not look like me, and I do not look like him. [10] He is 5 feet 10 inches and has dark brown hair and a mustache, but I am 5 feet 8 inches with light brown hair and no mustache. [11] We will both wear shirts. [12] We predict that many of the students may not realize that they have interacted with two different people.

---

1. In sentence 1, change *I* to *my research partner and I,* since it is a joint project.

2. In sentence 1, change *copy* to the more formal word *recreate.*

3. The phrase *the change blindness experiment* is repeated in sentences 1 and 2. In sentence 2, replace it with *this experiment* because the word *this* helps connect ideas between sentences..

4. Sentences 4 and 5 are sequential actions. Combine them. Begin with the word *when* and change the second *pencil* to *it.* Be careful with verbs.

5. In sentence 7, add the introductory clause *After the student leaves* and a comma to the beginning of sentence.

6. Sentence 9 is wordy. Rewrite it so that it has only one clause and the phrase *each other.* Then change *look like* to *resemble.*

7. In sentence 10, replace *but* with *while* to emphasize the contrast.

8. Begin sentence 11 with *in addition* and a comma to show that this is additional information.

9. Add the adjective *different* to sentence 11 to emphasize that the students will not look alike.

10. Change *may* to *will* to show the strong certainty of the prediction.

ACTIVITY 10   Original Writing

On a separate sheet of paper, write a paragraph (at least six sentences) about a future event or situation you think will occur. Use at least two examples of future forms and underline them; try to use three if possible.

Here are some examples of how to begin.

- *There are several ways that technology may change education in the future.*
- *Future air travel will differ greatly from air travel today in a number of ways.*
- *In the future, people living in coastal areas will face multiple challenges as a result of rising sea levels.*

A farmer shakes apples from a tree in the Duchy of Cornwall, England.

5 Writing with Prepositions

WHAT DO YOU KNOW?

DISCUSS Look at the photo and read the caption. Discuss the questions.

1. What are the health benefits of eating apples?

2. What other foods and activities promote good health?

FIND THE ERRORS This paragraph contains two errors with a preposition. Find the errors and correct them. Explain your corrections to a partner.

CAUSE-EFFECT PARAGRAPH

An Apple a Day

[1] A famous proverb says "An apple a day keeps the doctor away," but how true is this statement today? [2] The earliest written record of this saying was at the 1860s. [3] More than 150 years later, we now have scientific evidence that eating apples can improve our health. [4] In a 2004 study by the United States Department of Agriculture, apples were the twelfth best food for antioxidants, which help fight diseases. [5] Apples are also good for our digestion because they are full by fiber. [6] In addition, researchers believe that phloridizin, which is found only in apples, can help make stronger bones. [7] In 2015, *Medical News Today* ranked apples first on its list of the top ten healthy foods to eat, which means that apples were ranked better for our health than almonds, broccoli, blueberries, and oily fish. [8] Some people might think it is difficult to eat an apple every day, but others recognize the great health benefits of eating this delicious fruit.

Grammar Forms

5.1 Prepositions and Prepositional Phrases

Type	Example	Example Sentence
Single-word prepositions	about from to after in with at of without before on for since	Trees **in** urban areas reduce air pollution and provide habitats **for** urban wildlife.
Multi-word prepositions	because of due to in spite of instead of with regard to	Officials closed the bridge **due to** safety concerns.
Prepositional phrases (prep. + object)	at the highest point due to this for this reason in the 1800s on the anniversary	**In 1871**, the Great Chicago Fire killed almost 300 people, and thousands more were homeless **due to this tragedy.**

Notes

1. A preposition and its object is called a prepositional phrase. The object can be a noun or noun phrase.
2. Some prepositional phrases can occur in different parts of sentences. At the beginning of a sentence, a prepositional phrase is usually followed by a comma.

    In the winter, most bears hibernate.

    Most bears hibernate **in the winter**.

ACTIVITY 1

Underline the prepositions in each sentence.

1. Many businesses are not giving employee salary raises at this time due to a lack of funding.

2. Many employees at the Riviera Bank lost their jobs after the National Bank purchased the Riviera Bank in November.

3. In the last decade, temperatures at the North Pole have been unusually warm.

4. One of the greatest health threats in the United States is skin cancer.

5. The article discusses the differences in laws with regard to e-cigarettes.

6. In Alaska, the Northern Lights, or Aurora Borealis, are often visible in the winter because of the extreme darkness.

7. The new transportation report shows the growth in the number of people taking the new buses from the city center.

8. Spanish, which started in the Castile region of Spain, is an example of a Romance language.

ACTIVITY 2

Underline the prepositional phrases in the sentences below. Some sentences have more than one prepositional phrase.

1. The government announced that unemployment was at its lowest point in the last decade.

2. Recent research shows that people remember information that they read in print format better than information they read in digital format.

3. The inspectors found that many bridges that were built before the early 1900s needed repairs.

4. Most international students experience culture shock. For this reason, these students should learn about culture shock.

5. In the United States, most public holidays are on Mondays rather than on the anniversaries of the events they honor.

6. A cupcake with icing may contain up to 300 calories.

Common Uses

Prepositions and prepositional phrases are necessary in all types of writing. They are often used to clarify ideas or to express specific information. They are used:

1. to show location	**above** Germany / **at** school / **by** the sea / **in** Florida **near** an urban center / **on** the Internet
2. to show time	**as** soon as possible / **at** night / **for** three days / **in** May **in** the morning / **since** 2012
3. to show direction or movement	**along** the coast / **down** the road / **into** the woods **out** of town / **to** the moon / **up** the hill
4. to show a logical relationship	**according to** the boss / **because of** the problem **in case of** an accident / **instead of** the first idea **rather than** the original plan / **without** becoming a problem

Note
In academic writing, subjects are often followed by prepositional phrases. The verb agrees with the subject, not the object of the preposition.

People **in the back of a large room** often have difficulty seeing a presenter's slides.

Prepositions commonly occur in combination with other words. They are used:

1. with certain nouns noun + prep.	One **advantage of the first plan** is its lower cost. The **reason for replacing** the two elements is explained in the following chapter.
2. with certain verbs verb + prep.	In today's economy, it is difficult for parents to **provide for their families**. Of the university entrance exams that students take today, only a few **concentrate on testing** critical thinking skills.
3. with certain adjectives adj. + prep.	A few engineers are **concerned about the trend** in some cities toward extremely tall buildings. Many consumers are not **interested in completing** online surveys.

Read each sentence. Underline the correct preposition in the parentheses.

1. The directions say to put this type of medication directly (*at* / *on*) the wound.

2. When reading an article or text book on the Internet (*from* / *instead of*) in print, people tend to skim rather than to read deeply.

3. While most ducklings will follow their mothers (*into* / *at*) the water, a few may wait for a push from an adult duck.

4. The lack of advance planning resulted (*of* / *in*) several critical errors in the experiment.

5. Some teachers prefer when students apologize for being late to class (*during* / *as soon as*) they enter, while others see it as a disruption and would rather students come into class quietly.

6. The numbers (*at* / *with*) the top of the graph demonstrate a strong need for smaller classes in our schools.

7. Often one solution to traffic and parking problems is to add new bus routes (*into* / *at*) the city center.

8. (*On* / *In*) the winter, the squirrels eat the nuts they gathered during the fall.

ACTIVITY 4

Fill in the blanks with the correct phrase from the word box.

accuses you of	be addicted to	interested in	the current problem of (*use twice*)
a major source of	consists of	resulted in	

1. The report did not address _____ insufficient college scholarships.

2. The problems in the 1997 election _____ changes in voting procedures.

3. It seems to be more common for boys than girls to _____ video games.

4. Jackie Evancho, an American pop singer, became _____ singing after seeing the movie *The Phantom of the Opera*.

5. Online advertising is _____ income for a company such as Facebook.

6. Flavoring popcorn is simple because it _____ adding butter or salt.

7. If someone _____ committing a crime, you should contact a lawyer at once.

8. After living in other countries, it can be hard to understand _____ the high cost of medical care in the United States when it is so much lower in other places.

Common Errors

Common Error 5.1 Is the preposition correct?

One problem ~~for~~ *with* living downtown is that there are not usually many places to park on the streets.

REMEMBER: When you read, notice how prepositions are used. When writing, if you are unsure of which preposition to use, look in a dictionary or on the Internet.

ACTIVITY 5 **Common Error 5.1**

Read each sentence. Underline the correct preposition (or Ø for no preposition) in parentheses.

1. The brightness (*for* / *of* / *with*) the night stars and especially the Milky Way depends on the amount of street lighting (*at* / *in* / *on*) the area.

2. The biology labs are usually closed (*in* / *on* / *since*) the weekends, but someone has to come in at some point to feed the animals.

3. Essay exams can be very useful tests (*by* / *for* / *to*) history teachers to find out if students can explain why a certain event happened (*at* / *in* / *on*) a certain year.

4. The number of teenage smokers has not changed significantly (*since* / *in* / *Ø*) the last five years.

5. When one person becomes legally married (*for* / *to* / *Ø*) another, those people have new legal obligations (*for* / *in* / *to*) the rest of their lives.

6. The judge told the defendants that they would hear the decision of the court (*in* / *after* / *Ø*) exactly two months.

7. The Great Depression (*at* / *in* / *on*) the United States was (*between* / *during* / *Ø*) the years (*at* / *in* / *of*) 1929 and 1939, which means it was a decade of economic despair.

8. Although that area used to be one of the resting points for the migrating butterflies, they stopped coming there (*before 20 years* / *20 years ago* / *from 20 years*).

Common Error 5.2 Does the verb after a prepositional phrase agree with the subject?

are
According to the report, this year's exam scores from Westport High School ~~is~~ higher than ever before.

has
The President of the United States ~~have~~ the power to veto a bill that Congress passes.

REMEMBER: The verb following an object of a preposition agrees with the subject of the sentence, not the object of the prepositional phrase.

ACTIVITY 6   Common Error 5.2 ✓

In each sentence, circle the correct verb form in parentheses.

1.   Having two or three computer monitors per computer (**is** / *are*) the norm now in many offices. Although this is more expensive to maintain, it is worth the expense because studies have shown that office workers with one monitor (**get** / *gets*) distracted more easily clicking between tabs than they do when moving between monitors.

2.   All people in the world (**need** / *needs*) the same basic things. We all need shelter, food, and companionship. Unfortunately, homeless people have to find a way to survive without all of these things. In many large cities, homelessness (**is** / *are*) an especially serious problem.

3.   The states in the middle of the United States (*is* / **are**) called the Bread Basket because most of the country's wheat (*come* / **comes**) from this area. In fact, the amount of wheat from these states (**is** / *are*) enough to make billions of loaves of bread annually.

4.   Cell phones are a convenient way to communicate with one another. However, cell phones in the hands of children (**have** / *has*) many other important uses as well. Children in some countries in Africa (**learn** / *learns*) to read on cell phones because cell phones can be easier to get than books. Another use for cell phones (**is** / *are*) medical. Doctors in some developing countries (**use** / *uses*) cell phones to provide health care.

Common Error 5.3 Is the preposition combination correct?

of   *about*
The lack ~~for~~ human emotion in text messages sometimes caused readers to become confused ~~in~~ the writer's true message, but emojis have helped overcome this problem.

REMEMBER: Prepositions can be combined with certain nouns, verbs, and adjectives. When you see these preposition combinations, try to notice the words that go together. When writing, if you are unsure of your preposition combination, look in a dictionary.

ACTIVITY 7   **Common Error 5.3** ✓

Read the following sentences. Underline the correct word or phrase in parentheses.

1. Some therapists are recommending coloring books for adults as a type of relaxation therapy. They say the books work well (*because* / *because of* / *because with*) the focus that they provide.
   don't like / don't agree   p.62 p.221

2. Some doctors are opposed (*to* / *for* / *with*) the idea of our obtaining much of our nutrition (*between* / *from* / *in*) pills or other supplements instead of real food.

3. Small observatories usually (*consist in* / *consist* / *consist of*) only one telescope, while Mauna Kea, the largest observatory in the world, has 13 telescopes.

4. Government tax reductions (*help* / *help by* / *help on*) wind power to compete (*with* / *as* / *to*) coal, gas, and nuclear energy.

5. The Chinese are drinking more milk than ever before. (*At* / *For* / *With*) this reason, they need more cows and more grass to feed those cows. China does not have enough grass, so they rely (*on* / *in* / *about*) imports of hay from the United States.

6. Some paintings look very different depending (*on* / *at* / *in*) how far (*in front of* / *at front for* / *in front*) the painting the viewer stands.

7. When discussing something important, it can be better to talk face-to-face (*instead of* / *instead* / *instead for*) texting. Texting can result (*of* / *in* / *about*) unexpected miscommunications.

8. Table 2 illustrates the differences (*by* / *of* / *in*) the success rates of boys and girls with regard (*to* / *of* / *in*) middle school and high school science classes.

Academic Vocabulary

Adjective + Preposition Combinations Frequently Used in Academic Writing

associated with	capable of	different from	known as	responsible for
aware of	concerned about	interested in	related to	similar to

Source: Corpus of Contemporary American English (Davies 2008–)

ACTIVITY 8   **Vocabulary in Academic Writing**

Use the academic vocabulary to complete the sentences. For some sentences, more than one answer is possible.

Subject Area	Example from Academic Writing
Urban Studies	**1.** The citizens' questions about building new hotels in their city are _____ their questions about other new development plans.
English Literature	**2.** Reading about other people's choices in different situations can help people become more _____ their own life choices.
Sociology	**3.** Sociologists who study the roles of women in different cultures consider the attitudes _____ their positions at home and at work.
Economics	**4.** Credit card debt is very _____ other kinds of debt because not paying credit card bills can cause long-term financial problems.
Psychology	**5.** Freud's theories about the unconscious mind's influence on human behavior are very closely _____ his theories about human instincts.
Biology	**6.** The study of fish and other creatures in lakes and oceans is _____ *aquatic biomonitoring.*
Public Health	**7.** The local government is _____ the long waits and the low quality of care in the new neighborhood clinics.
Education	**8.** The tutors are generally _____ helping the writing students improve their second drafts.
Business Management	**9.** Everyone hoped that the young CEO was _____ running his father's business.
History	**10.** The first colonists in America were _____ learning from the Native Americans. They especially wanted to know which crops to grow.

Put It Together

ACTIVITY 8 **Review Quiz**

Multiple Choice Choose the letter of the correct answer.

1. Martin Luther King was interested _____ improving the lives of African-Americans everywhere, but he wanted that change to take place without violence.

    a. to **b.** in **c.** for **d.** with

2. Although parents want to help their children with their math homework, most parents are not familiar _____ the type of math their children are learning in school these days.

    a. in **b.** of **c.** to **d.** with

3. The new law will take effect next year, but many remain opposed _____ it.

    a. by **b.** from **c.** to **d.** with

4. Although it is hard to know how easy it will be to find jobs in many professions in the future, it is certain that there will always be a need _____ health care workers.

    a. with **b.** of **c.** in **d.** for

5. In spite _____ the country's dry climate, most of the land is relatively green.

    a. as **b.** in **c.** of **d.** to

Error Correction One of the five underlined words or phrases is not correct. Find the error and correct it. Be prepared to explain your answer.

6. Swans are not <u>only</u> very beautiful and graceful birds, but they <u>are</u> also very loyal animals. Most swans find a mate and <u>stay</u> together <u>since</u> many years, sometimes <u>even</u> for life.

7. Procrastinators are not <u>particular</u> lazy. <u>In fact</u>, they can <u>be</u> quite hardworking and creative people. They usually have no trouble finding <u>a lot of</u> things to do, as long as it is not the one thing that they are supposed to <u>be doing</u>.

8. <u>Becoming</u> physically fit is one <u>of</u> the many <u>ways</u> that people can benefit <u>from play</u> sports. In addition, sports are <u>beneficial</u> for people's mental and emotional health.

The northern lights glow in Norway.

Building Greater Sentences

Combine these short sentences into one sentence. You can add new words and move words around, but you should not add or omit any ideas. More than one answer is possible, but these sentences require a prepositional phrase or preposition combination.

1. a. The northern lights appear in Norway.
   b. They are in the northern region.
   c. Northern lights appear in late autumn.
   d. They also appear in winter and early spring.

_____

_____

2. a. Products are located near the front.
   b. Products are in supermarkets.
   c. These products sell more quickly.
   d. This is generally true.
   e. This is because of their location.

_____

_____

3. a. Twitter is very popular now.
   b. Twitter is popular all over the world.
   c. There are hundreds of millions of tweets a day.
   d. There are hundreds of billions of tweets a year.

_____

_____

Read the paragraph. Then follow the directions in the 10 steps to edit the information and composition of this paragraph. Write your revised paragraph on a separate sheet of paper. Be careful with capitalization and punctuation. Check your answers with the class.

COMPARISON PARAGRAPH

How Cultures View Aging

[1] Different cultures look at the process of aging in different ways. [2] In some cultures, youth is admired and aging is feared. [3] People try to hide the fact that they are aging in a variety of different ways. [4] Some people color their hair in order to hide the gray. [5] Others go to even more extreme lengths and have plastic surgery on their faces and bodies to appear younger than they are. [6] Older people who can no longer take care of themselves often move to homes or communities where professional caretakers can care for them. [7] In other cultures, however, things are very different. [8] Age is respected rather than feared. [9] People in those cultures tend to think of older people as smart and worthy of respect. [10] The wrinkles on their faces are seen as symbols of valuable experience rather than simply as fading beauty. [11] In these cultures, people do not put their aging parents in special homes or hospitals. [12] They often bring them into their own homes and care for them themselves.

1. In sentence 1, change *look* to the more academic word *view*. Make any other necessary changes.

2. It is not good to repeat the same word too often. Find the adjective that is repeated in sentence 1. The second time it is used, change it to another suitable adjective.

3. In sentence 2, the word *some* is not specific. Change it to *many western*.

4. In sentence 5, change *and have* to *by having*

5. Sentences 4 and 5 are examples of sentence 3. Connect the sentences with *and*. Begin the new sentence with *For example*.

6. In sentence 6, put *In addition* at the beginning of the sentence.

7. The phase *older people* is used twice in the paragraph. In sentence 6, change it to *senior citizens*.

8. It is good to add specific examples. In sentence 7, add the phrase *such as many eastern societies* after *cultures*.

9. In sentence 9, change *smart* to a more specific adjective meaning intelligence gained from experience.

10. Connect sentences 11 and 12. Add this phrase in the best location: *instead of.* Consider changing verb forms and punctuation.

ACTIVITY 11   Original Writing

On a separate sheet of paper, write a comparison paragraph (at least six sentences) about a topic related to health. Use at least two prepositional phrases and one preposition combination, and underline them.

Here are some examples of how to begin.

- *In spite of what most people think, fast walking is actually better for your body than running.*
- *There are many popular diet plans, but there are several reasons why the Mediterranean plan is most commonly recommended by doctors.*
- *For a young person, playing soccer is better than playing American football for several reasons.*

A woman reads to her daughter in Russia.

6 Using Modals in Sentences

WHAT DO YOU KNOW?

DISCUSS Look at the photo and read the caption. Discuss the questions.

1. Did anyone read to you when you were a child? If so, who? What did they read to you?
2. Where and when did you learn to read? What do you remember about the experience?

FIND THE ERRORS This paragraph contains two errors with modals. Find the errors and correct them. Explain your corrections to a partner.

OPINION PARAGRAPH

The Best Age for Children to Learn to Read

[1] Children should start learning to read when they are ready rather than at a specific age or grade level. [2] Typically, in U.S. schools, children start learning to read at six years old, in first grade. [3] This works well for many children, but some children are not ready at this age. [4] For those children, being forced to read before they are ready can actually be harmful. [5] It can to cause children to lose confidence in their ability to read and in their ability to learn in general. [6] Experts agree that parents should expose babies and toddlers to books. [7] They also agree that parents should start reading to their children when they are still infants. [8] However, teachers should to encourage their students to read when they show interest rather than force them to read before they are ready.

Grammar Forms

6.1   Kinds of Modals

	Modals	Example (modal + verb)
Single-word modals	can might will could must would may should	Ducks **can fly** up to 60 miles per hour. In the future, all cars **could be** electric. Scientists **may find** a cure for cancer soon. Students **must take** a statistics class in their first year. It **would be** a mistake to disregard this research.
Phrasal modals	be able to be supposed to have to ought to	Ducks **are able to fly** up to 60 miles an hour. Freshmen **have to take** a composition class.

Notes

1. Use a modal with the base form of the verb.

   Most people **should eat** more fruit.

2. An adverb of frequency usually goes between the modal and the verb.

   People **should** <u>never</u> **text** while they are driving.

6.2   Modals: Negatives

Single-word Modals: Negatives

modal + *not* + verb • The modal *can* + *not* are joined as *cannot*.	Politicians **should not accept** large contributions. Legally, politicians **cannot accept** bribes.

Phrasal Modals: Negatives

do / does + *not* + *have to* + verb	Applicants **do not have to provide** references.
did + *not* + *have to* + verb	The witness **did not have to appear** before the court.
am / is / are + *not* + *able to* + verb	The manager **is not able to authorize** the budget.
was / were + *not* + *supposed to* + verb	The jury members **were not supposed to discuss** the trial.

Read each sentence. Underline the modals and the base forms of the verbs that follow them. In some sentences or questions, there is more than one modal + verb combination.

1. While some new medications may not cure serious diseases like cancer, they can help patients live longer.

2. New business owners must consider how much money they can safely invest in their businesses.

3. In most countries, professional athletes earn much higher pay than other professionals such as teachers, lawyers, and even doctors. Should athletes earn more money than other professionals?

4. In France, restaurants that serve more than 150 meals a day have to find a way to reduce the amount of food they throw away.

5. Laws that are useful now may have to change in order to keep up with the times.

6. In California, individuals cannot own beachfront property. This is because people there believe that everyone should have access to beaches, not just rich people.

7. Raising the speed limit on the highways to 75 miles per hour would not be a good idea.

8. In the past, women were supposed to stay home and take care of the children instead of work.

Underline the correct modal forms.

1. Many employers say telecommuting more than twice a week (_would not be_ / _would be not_) a good idea.

2. Most people surveyed said politicians (_should be always_ / _should always be_) honest.

3. Humans landing on Mars (_might not_ / _might to not_) be possible now, but it is likely to happen eventually.

4. Cars in the United States (_did not have to_ / _had not to_) have seatbelts until 1968.

5. A large increase in the price of gas (_might result_ / _might be result_) in fewer cars on the highways.

6. Meditation (_can help often_ / _can often help_) reduce anxiety.

7. Teachers (_should to use_ / _should use_) some games in the classroom because they (_can_ / _can to_) help some students learn faster and more effectively.

8. People with diabetes are (_not supposed to_ / _supposed not to_) eat sugar.

Common Uses

6.3 Using Modals

Modals are auxiliary (helping) verbs that change the meaning of other verbs. They can express ability, opinion, possibility, expectation, prohibition, or necessity. They can also express degrees of certainty. Modals are used in academic writing:

1. to express present or past ability or capability (*can, could, be able to*)	Some animals **can predict** earthquakes up to five days before one happens.
	An Italian scientist said he **was able to predict** the L'Aquila earthquake by measuring the changes in radon gas.
2. to give an opinion or state a conclusion (*should, will, ought to, must*) • This use is common in argumentative or opinion essays, especially in the thesis statement or conclusion.	In sum, 16-year-olds **should be able to vote** in national elections.
3. to hedge, or to make information sound less certain or direct (*may, can, could, might, should*) • Academic writers use hedging to soften their ideas or to acknowledge uncertainty.	Some people believe that urban farming **could solve** many of the world's hunger problems.
4. to express necessity or a requirement (*must, have to, ought to*) • Use *must* and *have to* for the present and future tenses. Use *had to* for the past tense. • The negative modals *must not* and *not have to* have different meanings. *Must not* refers to prohibition, and *not have to* refers to lack of necessity.	The dust storms last year were so bad that everyone **had to wear** masks on their faces. The researchers **must not reveal** the results of the experiment until they have analyzed all the data. Since they had enough data, the researchers **did not have to repeat** the experiment.
5. to express a future plan (*will*)	This paper **will compare** daily life in Tokyo with daily life in Beijing.

Notes
1. See Unit 4, Writing about the Future, for more information on *will*.
2. In academic writing, modals generally appear several times in a paragraph. There is rarely only one modal in a paragraph.

ACTIVITY 3 √

Read each sentence. Underline the correct modal in parentheses.

1. Many people think that elementary schools (<u>should</u> / may) provide more instruction on the dangers of tobacco.

2. Early cell phone batteries lasted longer than smartphone batteries. You (were not supposed to / <u>did not have to</u>) charge them every day.

3. People are living longer these days. More people (could / <u>should</u>) live to be over 100 in the future.

4. Early cell phones (<u>were not able to</u> / must not) connect to the Internet.

5. After the government passes the new carbon emission laws, all businesses (can / <u>will have to</u>) pay fines if they (<u>cannot</u> / must not) stay within the new limits.

6. I believe that students (<u>should not</u> / could not) wait until middle school to study a foreign language.

7. After Hurricane Katrina in 2005, people who lost their homes (<u>had to</u> / could) move to temporary housing outside of New Orleans.

8. After getting a speeding ticket, you (could / <u>must</u>) pay a fine within a specified amount of time.

ACTIVITY 4

Complete each sentence with your own ideas. Use a modal that expresses the purpose in parentheses.

1. Fifty years ago, people _____

   _____ (express ability in the past)

2. Most instructors believe that students _____

   _____ (give an opinion)

3. In the future, this city _____

   _____ (hedge)

4. To perform well on tests, students _____

   _____ (express a necessity)

5. Next month, _____

   _____ (express a future plan)

Common Errors

Common Error 6.1 Does the modal need *to*?

can cause

Drinking coffee in the late afternoon ~~can to cause~~ sleep problems.

to

People who have trouble sleeping have watch their coffee consumption.
^

REMEMBER: Single-word modals (such as *can, must,* or *should*) are followed by the base verb. Do not add *to*. However, phrasal modals (such as *have to, be able to, ought to*) include the word *to*.

ACTIVITY 5 **Common Error 6.1** ✓

Read the following sentences. Underline the modal and verb in each sentence. If the modal + verb form is correct, write *C* on the line. If it is wrong, write *X* on the line. Then write the correct modal and verb above the sentence.

X **1.** In the future, the development of new technologies may ~~to~~ continue to make work easier and better for employees in many different fields.

X **2.** Many parents believe that their children should ~~to~~ wear helmets when playing soccer to protect them from head injuries.

C **3.** Until the laws changed in the United States in 1978, women were not able to keep their jobs after they got pregnant.

X **4.** In 2008, Chinese Olympic officials were worried about rain on the opening and closing days of the Olympics. They seeded the clouds with silver iodide to make it rain early so there would ~~to~~ be no rain on those days.

X **5.** Although we recycle plastic, we must ~~to~~ find alternatives to plastic wherever possible.

C **6.** Some psychologists believe children are too busy these days and that they ought to have more free time on their own.

C **7.** Many students believe they have to complete internships in their field while they are still in school in order to get a job after they graduate.

X **8.** One function of a turtle's shell is to protect its head, but some turtles, such as Loggerhead turtles, cannot ~~to~~ put their heads into their shells.

Common Error 6.2 Is the negative form correct?

should not water

When there is a water shortage, homeowners ~~do not should water~~ their plants every day.

do not have to water

You ~~have not to water~~ some plants more than once a week.

REMEMBER: For negative single-word modals, put *not* between the modal and the base form of the verb. For phrasal modals, add *do, does,* or *did.*

ACTIVITY 6   **Common Error 6.2**   ✓

Fill in the blanks with the correct negative forms of the modals in parentheses.

1. The pockets in women's clothing have always been smaller than those in men's clothing. This may be because designers believed that women _____didn't need to_____ (*need to*) carry important things like wallets with them. Also, they often carried purses. Times have changed, though. I believe women ___should not have to___ (*should have to*) carry purses anymore. Women's pockets ___should not be___ (*should be*) smaller than men's pockets anymore.

2. Occasionally, drivers cause accidents by driving the wrong way on highways. Although wrong way driving ___may not be___ (*may be*) the biggest cause of accidents, it usually results in death. Scientists have created new sensors to put on cars to help solve this problem. Unfortunately, though, this technology ___may not be___ (*may be*) affordable for all.

3. You ___do not have to know___ (*have to know*) a lot about photography to take good pictures. However, knowing a few basic rules is helpful. One rule is that you ___should not center___ (*should center*) the subject of your photo. You should put the subject of your photo off-center and preferably in the top third of the photo instead.

4. Parents in many cultures often teach their children that they ___should not interrupt___ (*should interrupt*) when adults are talking. However, in cultures where interrupting is very common, if you do not interrupt, you ___may not ever get___ (*may ever get*) a chance to talk.

Common Error 6.3 Do you hedge correctly?

> *could cause*
> Skipping breakfast ~~causes~~ students to perform poorly in school.

> *Praise may motivate*
> ~~I think praise motivates~~ children more than criticism.

REMEMBER: Academic writers often use *may, might, can,* and *could* to hedge. They avoid conversational expressions such as *I think* or *maybe*.

ACTIVITY 7 **Common Error 6.3**

Restate these sentences with the hedging modals in parentheses.

1. I think some house plants are a dangerous addition to your home, especially if you have small children or pets. (*may*) _____

_____

2. Standing desks are becoming more and more popular, but many people with back pain are causing themselves problems by using them incorrectly. (*could*) _____

_____

3. The box jellyfish is the most poisonous fish in the ocean. (*might*) _____

_____

4. Though research connecting cell phone use with cancer shows little need for concern at this time, using a handset whenever possible is a good safety precaution. (*may*) _____

_____

5. Studies show that chewing sugar-free gum after eating helps to prevent tooth decay. (*could*) _____

_____

6. Facial recognition technology in airports is the best way to keep everyone safer and speed up the process of airport security. (*may*) _____

_____

7. Acupuncture helps children who have chronic pain. (*could*) _____

_____

8. While spending too much time playing video games is not healthy, video games are effective educational tools. (*may; could*) _____

_____

Academic Vocabulary

Modal + Verb Combinations Frequently Used in Academic Writing

can help	have to	might seem	should include	will continue to be
could do	may lead to	must take	should try to	would be

Source: Corpus of Contemporary American English (Davies 2008–)

ACTIVITY 8   **Vocabulary in Academic Writing**

Use the modal + verb combinations to complete the sentences.

Subject Area	Example from Academic Writing
Criminal Justice	**1.** To those who do not work in criminal justice, most of the important questions in the subject of criminology _____ simple.
Health	**2.** As a physical therapist, becoming familiar with each new patient's medical history _____ all previous injuries.
Political Science	**3.** If travelers need help in some foreign countries, their embassy _____ very little to help them.
Computer Science	**4.** Computer hacking has been a problem since the 1970s, and experts believe it _____ a problem for many more years.
Neuroscience	**5.** Exposure to lead _____ serious nerve and brain damage in children.
English Composition	**6.** Parents _____ teach young boys that it is acceptable to cry.
History	**7.** Historians often think about how the world _____ different if a king, president, or other leader had lived longer or died earlier.
Education	**8.** Teachers often tell their students that they _____ more responsibility for their own learning.
Social Work	**9.** One of the most difficult tasks for social workers is when they _____ take children away from their parents.
Natural Sciences	**10.** Learning to use the scientific method of inquiry _____ students learn to think more critically.

Put It Together

Multiple Choice Choose the letter of the correct answer.

1. A study determined that popular Wikipedia pages _____ be as accurate as an encyclopedia because hundreds or even thousands of readers have checked and edited them.

   a. should not   **b.** must not   **c.** may   **d.** will not

2. Effective advertisements _____ inform and educate as well as be memorable.

   a. might   **b.** could   **c.** may not   **d.** should

3. Pablo Picasso _____ finish his art school entrance examination in only one day, although he had one month to complete it.

   a. was able to   **b.** did not have to   **c.** could to   **d.** must not

4. Sleep experts say that people _____ sleepwalkers up, as it can cause them to feel confused and disoriented. It is best to simply lead them back to bed.

   a. should not wake   **b.** not should wake   **c.** should do not wake   **d.** do not should wake

5. According to new brain imaging studies, intense exercise _____ help people who suffer from some forms of depression.

   a. might   **b.** might be able   **c.** might able   **d.** might have

Error Correction One of the five underlined words or phrases is not correct. Find the error and correct it. Be prepared to explain your answer.

6. Nowadays, computers <u>can be able to</u> read people's body language from <u>computer users'</u> movements, <u>which</u> computer scientists are saying <u>could be</u> very helpful <u>in the development of</u> robots.

7. The scientists <u>who found</u> the Jurassic dinosaur eggs in China <u>in</u> 2010 <u>know</u> immediately that this discovery <u>would help</u> them <u>to</u> answer some important questions.

8. Three-dimensional printing <u>has become</u> a reality <u>faster than</u> many thought possible. Businesses <u>can now choose</u> from several different models, and experts think they <u>will soon</u> <u>to be</u> inexpensive enough for homeowners to purchase.

ACTIVITY 10 Building Greater Sentences

Combine these short sentences into one sentence. You can add new words and move words around, but you should not add or omit any ideas. More than one answer is possible, but these sentences require modals.

1. a. Honeybees are dying in huge numbers.
   b. Honeybees need our protection.
   c. Honeybees pollinate one-third of all food crops.
   d. Without honeybees, we may not have enough food to eat.

_____

_____

2. a. Many people love watching movies.
   b. For these people being a film critic may be the perfect job.
   c. Successful film critics need to know a lot about film making.
   d. Successful film critics also need to know a lot about journalism.

_____

_____

3. a. E-mail can be very distracting.
   b. Checking e-mail too often can prevent you from working efficiently.
   c. Experts say you should turn off the e-mail beep sound on your computer.
   d. The beep sound signals a new e-mail.

_____

_____

Read the paragraph. Then follow the directions in the 10 steps to edit the information and composition of this paragraph. Write your revised paragraph on a separate sheet of paper. Be careful with capitalization and punctuation. Check your answers with the class.

OPINION PARAGRAPH

The Future of Money

[1] Money is changing. [2] The money we use in the future will not exist in paper form at all. [3] People are using cash less and less. [4] People like to keep cash in their wallets for small purchases, but people use credit or debit cards for everything else. [5] Cryptocurrencies such as Bitcoin are the money of the future. [6] Bitcoin is already in use in various places such as Scandinavia. [7] Another alternative to cash and credit cards is the use of mobile payments. [8] With mobile payments, a smartphone acts like a credit card. [9] Before too long, credit cards and checks will probably be a thing of the past.

---

1. In sentence 1, add *and the way we use it* in the best location.

2. In sentence 2, *will not exist* is too strong because we do not know this for a fact. Hedge with the modal *might*.

3. Begin sentence 3 with *already* to show that this is an example of information in sentence 2.

4. In sentence 4, change *people* in the last clause to *most people* to hedge.

5. In sentence 4, change *use* to *prefer to use*.

6. In sentence 4, change *prefer* to *would prefer* as another hedge.

7. In sentence 5, the verb *are* is too strong because we cannot be 100 percent certain about the future. Add the modal *may* and change the verb form to hedge.

8. Sentence 6 is an example of the information in sentence 5. Begin sentence 6 with the phrase *in fact*.

9. In sentence 8, add the modal *can* and change the verb form if needed.

10. In sentence 9, add the word *cash* as the second item in the list.

On a separate sheet of paper, write an opinion paragraph (at least six sentences) about something you think is likely to change in the near future. Use at least one example of a modal and underline it; try to use two or more if possible.

Here are some examples of how to begin.

- *The world may be changing faster now than it ever has before.*
- *In the future, people may not travel in the same way they do now.*
- *The way people enjoy music might change considerably in the next 10 years.*

Brazilian mural artist Eduardo Kobra paints the side of a 184-foot (56-meter) high building in São Paulo, Brazil.

7 Using Adjective Clauses

WHAT DO YOU KNOW?

DISCUSS Look at the photo and read the caption. Discuss the questions.

1. Do you think public art is important? Why, or why not?

2. Describe a mural, statue, or other piece of public art in your home city or town.

FIND THE ERRORS This paragraph contains two errors with adjective clauses. Find the errors and correct them. Explain your corrections to a partner.

DESCRIPTIVE PARAGRAPH

Eduardo Kobra

¹Eduardo Kobra is a famous Brazilian street artist which paints enormous murals on buildings. ²Kobra is famous for his use of very bright colors. ³He is also known for repeated patterns that make his paintings resemble giant kaleidoscopes. ⁴His patterns often use geometric shapes such as squares, circles, and triangles. ⁵In addition, some of Kobra's murals are three-dimensional. ⁶Many of Kobra's murals are portraits of famous people from different time periods and parts of the world. ⁷Kobra also paints scenes make statements about topics such as war, pollution, deforestation, and other important social issues. ⁸In addition to Brazil, his colorful murals are on city walls in the United States, Russia, Japan, and many European countries.

Grammar Forms

7.1   Adjective Clauses

An adjective clause (also called a relative clause) has a subject and a verb. The clause can begin with the relative pronoun *who*, *which*, *that*, or *whom*. An adjective clause follows the noun, noun phrase, or pronoun it describes.

1. The relative pronoun can be a subject.

a. *who* or *that* for people	Middle-aged people **who** <u>exercise</u> tend to have fewer severe health S V problems later in life.
b. *that* or *which* for things	More consumers are buying vehicles **that** <u>use electricity</u>. S V
c. *which* for things in a nonrestrictive clause	The Nissan Leaf, **which** <u>was introduced in 2010</u>, is an all-electric car. S V
d. *who* for people in a nonrestrictive clause	Nelson Mandela, **who** <u>died in 2013</u>, was president of South Africa from S V 1994 to 1999.

2. The relative pronoun can be an object of a verb.

a. *whom* or *that* for people	This is the man **whom** <u>officials believe</u> stole the information. REL PRO S V
b. *which* or *that* for things	Scientists are developing a vitamin **that** <u>people will take only once a week</u>. REL PRO S V

3. The relative pronoun can be an object of a preposition.

a. preposition + *whom* for people	In some cultures, you should make eye contact with the person **to whom** <u>you are talking</u>. REL PRO S V
b. preposition + *which* for things	They conducted a study **in which** <u>they surveyed young coffee drinkers</u>. REL PRO S V

Notes

1. The subject pronoun *that* is more commonly used than *which*.
2. An adjective clause with nonessential information (also called a nonrestrictive clause) is separated from the independent clause with commas. You can delete the information from the sentence and still have the main idea.

    Tallahassee, <u>which is in north Florida</u>, is the state's capital.
3. An adjective clause with essential information (also called a restrictive clause) cannot be deleted without losing important meaning.

    The city <u>that we studied</u> was ancient.
4. The object pronoun is often omitted in academic writing.

    Scientists are developing a vitamin (that) people will take only once a week.

    Surprisingly, the person (whom) most voters preferred did not win the election.
5. *Whom* refers to the object of the main clause, not the subject. The use of *whom* is optional in most writing, but it is preferred in academic writing.

ACTIVITY 1

Underline each adjective clause. Some sentences have more than one adjective clause.

1. In 1986, the United States Congress passed the Computer Fraud and Abuse Act, which made computer hacking a crime.

2. The main purpose of this paper is to present key information from a recent study that showed that infants see colors differently from older people.

3. The Taj Mahal, which the Emperor Shah Jahan built in 1632 for his dead wife, is one of the best examples of Mughal architecture.

4. The planet Venus is the only planet which has days that are longer than its years.

5. Sea turtles are reptiles that marine biologists are fighting to protect.

6. Astronaut Scott Kelley, who has a twin brother who is also an astronaut, spent 340 days on the International Space Station.

7. There is a famous memorial in Berlin for the 96 German politicians who tried to stop Hitler in 1933.

8. Some doctors are prescribing meditation along with prescription medications for their patients for whom high blood pressure is a problem.

9. *Rashomon*, for which film director Akira Kurosawa is perhaps most famous, premiered in Tokyo in August of 1950.

10. The state of Louisiana includes 2,482 islands that cover nearly 1.3 million acres.

Underline the correct relative pronoun.

1. The students in the classes (*that / who*) had teacher's aides all passed the final exam.

2. Rosa Parks is the woman (*who / whom*) some call "the first lady of civil rights."

3. In 1961, the German Democratic Republic built a wall (*that / whom*) divided the city of Berlin into two cities.

4. The new lecturer was not aware that the person (*with whom / with who*) he shared an office was a concert pianist.

5. Some people (*whom / who*) get migraines started getting them when they were very young children.

6. DNA studies have proved that giraffes, (*that / which*) used to be considered one species, actually consist of four different species.

7. Italian, German, and French are the three languages (*in which / that*) most operas are written.

8. Modern techniques of recording brain activity are helping scientists to answer questions (*to whom / that*) people have been asking for hundreds of years.

Artists at Indiana University paint brain sculptures to raise awareness about brain health

Common Uses

7.2 Using Adjective Clauses

Adjective clauses are commonly used in academic writing. They describe, define, identify, or give additional details about nouns or pronouns. Use them:

1. to combine short sentences into one sentence	Redwood trees grow mainly on the Pacific coast from Oregon to California. + Redwood trees are the tallest trees in the world. = Redwood trees, **which are the tallest trees in the world**, grow mainly on the Pacific coast from Oregon to California.
2. to add information about a noun	The bark of the redwood tree contains chemicals **that protect the tree from insects**.
3. to add extra information	The coast redwood tree, **which is the same height as a 37-story building**, is the tallest type of redwood tree.

Note

Use *who*, *that*, or *which* for essential information. Use *which* or *who* with nonessential information and separate the adjective clause from the rest of the sentence with commas.

ACTIVITY 3

Underline the adjective clauses. Write *E* on the line if the information is essential and *NE* if it is nonessential. There may be more than one adjective clause in a sentence.

_NE_ **1.** Chlorophyll, which makes plants green, is a biomolecule that allows plants to absorb energy from light.

_E_ **2.** Linguists are working with native tribes that have languages that are disappearing.

_E_ **3.** There are now various genealogy Web sites that help people discover family members and ancestors of whom they have no knowledge.

_NE_ **4.** Abraham Lincoln, who had a wife from a slave-owning family, was the U.S. president who was responsible for making slavery illegal.

_E_ **5.** People who are irrationally afraid of spiders have a phobia that is called arachnophobia.

_E_ **6.** Genetics is the field of biology which may hold important answers to questions about hereditary diseases and their cures.

_E_ **7.** Social media Web sites are particularly useful for finding old friends with whom people have not had any contact in many years.

_NE_ **8.** Professor Denke, who is one of the authors of our history textbook, makes the subject interesting and important by connecting the past with the present and the future.

Common Errors

Common Error 7.1 Do you use *which*, *who*, or *that*?

> who / that
> Because of housing shortages in Shanghai, single Chinese people ~~which~~ are from other cities in China
> are not allowed to buy property there.
>
> which
> Amphibians, ~~that~~ are animals that can breathe on land and in the water, are cold-blooded.

REMEMBER: • In essential adjective clauses, use *who* or *that* to refer to people. Use *that* or *which* for things.
   • In nonessential adjective clauses, use *who* for people and *which* for things.

ACTIVITY 4   Common Error 7.1

Fill in the blanks with *which, who,* or *that*. More than one answer may be possible.

1. The Athabascans, _____who_____ are the original Alaskans, are not considered Eskimos like the Inupiat and Yup'ik.

2. Most dried fruits contain the same vitamins and nutrients as their nondried counterparts, with the exception of raisins, _____which_____ are lower in vitamin C than grapes.

3. Great managers are people _____who/that_____ can delegate, encourage, and give credit to those employees ____who/that____ deserve it.

4. Many people believe the myth _____that/which_____ people only use 10 percent of their brains.

5. Vitamin D, _____which_____ people need for healthy bones and teeth, comes from exposure to sunlight.

6. Forest kindergartens are schools _____that/which_____ are outside in nature, usually in forests.

7. Clouds are simply a gathering of very small droplets of water or crystals of ice _____that/which_____ are so light they can float in the air.

8. It is important to drink lots of water, _____which_____ comprises almost two-thirds of the body.

Common Error 7.2 Does the adjective clause need a comma?

Abraham Lincoln, who was the 16th president, was the first U.S. president to be assassinated.

who made owning slaves illegal

Abraham Lincoln was the president, ~~who made owning slaves illegal~~.

REMEMBER:
- Use commas around adjective clauses with additional, non-essential details.
- Do not use commas around essential information. To determine if the information is essential, take it out of the sentence. Then check if the sentence still makes sense.

ACTIVITY 5 Common Error 7.2

Read each paragraph. Underline the adjective clauses. Then add commas before and after the nonessential adjective clauses.

1. The lima bean plant has developed a special protection against caterpillars that eat the plant. When caterpillars start to eat the lima bean plant, the leaves release a special scent. This scent which smells very good alerts other nearby plants of the caterpillar danger. Then all the lima bean plants together release the same strong scent. This scent attracts wasps which are a natural enemy of the caterpillars. The wasps save the lima bean plants by killing the caterpillars.

2. Alcatraz Island which consists mainly of rock is a very small island in the middle of San Francisco Bay. It is just a little over one mile from the San Francisco shore. At first, Alcatraz was a lighthouse, but for 30 years it was a federal prison from which escape was almost impossible. To escape, prisoners needed to be very good swimmers. This is because the water around Alcatraz Island which is very cold and has very strong currents has Great White sharks in it. Now Alcatraz is a popular park which people can reach by ferry.

3. Computer Network Engineering is a relatively new field of Information Technology. Computer network engineers who are also referred to as network architects are the people who design and plan computer networks. They are not the network administrators whom people call if they have computer problems. A computer network engineer often has a specialized certificate in addition to an undergraduate degree in network administration or computer science.

4. The first woman to travel into space, Valentina Tereshkova, was a Russian cosmonaut. Tereshkova who was a factory worker when she applied to be a cosmonaut was hired as a cosmonaut partly because she was also an expert skydiver. Tereshkova's trip into space was in the Vostok 6 which launched June 16, 1963.

Common Error 7.3   Does the adjective clause have a subject pronoun?

> who
> The students improved the most were the ones from bilingual families.
> ^

REMEMBER: An adjective clause needs a subject pronoun.

ACTIVITY 6   Common Error 7.3

These sentences are missing the subject pronoun. Write the correct subject pronoun in the correct location. Choose from the box below.

in which	which	who (*use twice*)

1. Malala Yousafzai, *who* the Pakistani girl was shot on her way home from school, received the Nobel Peace Prize in 2014.

2. The dot-com bubble (1997–2000) refers to a period of time *in which* many new Internet companies opened up and succeeded.

3. Tex-Mex food is a type of food *which* combines Mexican and American ingredients.

4. Vegans are vegetarians *who* do not eat eggs or any dairy products.

Common Error 7.4   Is there an extra object pronoun?

> The research that the scientists did ~~it~~ was not used.

REMEMBER: Do not add object pronouns (*me, you, him, her, it, us,* or *them*) to adjective clauses.

ACTIVITY 7   Common Error 7.4

These sentences all have an extra object pronoun. Cross out the extra object pronoun.

1. The word *blue* can mean a color or it can mean *unhappy*, but the meaning that native-speaking children learn ~~it~~ first is a color.

2. Many people are concerned about the amount of food that restaurants and supermarkets discard ~~it~~.

3. The chemicals that companies put ~~them~~ into cleaning products and cosmetics to make ~~them~~ smell better can cause some people to have health problems.

4. New research supports the theory, which no one has been able to prove ~~it~~ so far, that brain size relative to body size indicates something about intelligence.

Academic Vocabulary

Words from the Academic Word List (Sublists 4 and 5)

access	alter	conflicts	phases	prior
adequate	challenge	exposure	precise	trends

Source: Academic Word List (Coxhead 2000)

ACTIVITY 8 **Vocabulary in Academic Writing**

Use the academic vocabulary to complete the sentences.

Subject Area	Example from Academic Writing
Psychology	**1.** SAD, or Seasonal Affective Disorder, is a type of depression that some people tend to have in the fall and winter when there is less opportunity for _____ to natural sunlight.
Geography	**2.** In 2009, it was reported that 25 percent of the world's population still lacked _____ to electricity, which means that they had to use wood and charcoal as their main sources of energy.
Neurology	**3.** Brain scientists are experimenting with new strategies that include attempting to _____ painful memories of people such as returning soldiers or victims of violent crime who have traumatic memories.
Environmental Science	**4.** In dry climates, one way to save water is to use a watering system called drip irrigation, which is a way of giving plants a very _____ amount of water.
Nursing	**5.** Focusing on patient safety, which is one of the current _____ in nursing education programs, has improved health care for all.
Astronomy	**6.** Although astronomers divide the _____ of the moon into eight categories, most people are only aware of four, which are the full moon, quarter moon, half moon, and new moon.
Business	**7.** Although on average Americans change their jobs every four to five years, they are staying in their jobs longer now than in _____ decades, which may be due to increased difficulty of finding a new job.
Music History	**8.** Beethoven did not let his biggest _____, which was that he was slowly going deaf, stop him from creating some of his most beautiful symphonies.
Education	**9.** Progressive education encourages teaching children to get along, which requires teaching students how to resolve _____ without fighting.
Statistics	**10.** Sometimes scientists first test a hypothesis with a small sample size. If the experiment is successful, they repeat it with a larger sample size that is statistically _____.

Put It Together

ACTIVITY 9 **Review Quiz**

Multiple Choice Choose the letter of the correct answer.

1. The Great Wall of China, _____ was built for defense, was not very effective for that purpose.

   a. whom **b.** which **c.** that **d.** it

2. Niagara Falls, _____ really three separate waterfalls, is in two different countries—Canada and the United States.

   a. which **b.** that is **c.** that were **d.** which is

3. People _____ allergies are worse in the spring could have hay fever.

   a. to whom **b.** who **c.** for whom **d.** for who

4. There is new brain wave research _____ how people actually remember their dreams.

   a. that explains **b.** which explains it **c.** is explains **d.** who explains

5. People _____ need only four hours of sleep each night are called *short sleepers*.

   a. for whom **b.** which **c.** that **d.** whom *only for object*

Error Correction One of the five underlined words or phrases is not correct. Find the error and correct it. Be prepared to explain your answer.

6. Many islands that have volcanoes on them have some very beautiful black sand
   which
   beaches, that often become uncomfortably hot in the summer sun.

7. Ninety-five percent of the cables, which connect countries to the Internet are at the
   no comma!
   bottom of the ocean.

8. Although gardening can be hard physical work, many people say that it is a hobby= *thing*
   which
   who they find very relaxing mentally.
   that
   ∅

Building Greater Sentences

Combine these short sentences into one sentence. You can add new words and move words around, but you should not add or omit any ideas. More than one answer is possible, but all of these sentences require adjective clauses.

1. **a.** There are about 5,000 stars that people can see from Earth.
   b. They can only see very bright stars without a telescope.
   c. Almost all of these stars are brighter than the sun.

   _____

   _____

2. **a.** ACL injuries are injuries to the knee.
   b. These injuries can end an athlete's career.
   c. These injuries happen twice as often to female athletes as to male athletes.

   _____

   _____

3. **a.** Nelson Mandela became South Africa's first black president.
   b. Nelson Mandela died in 2013.
   c. Nelson Mandela spent 27 years in prison before he became the president.

   _____

   _____

Read the paragraph. Then follow the directions in the 10 steps to edit the information and composition of this paragraph. Write your revised paragraph on a separate sheet of paper. Be careful with capitalization and punctuation. Check your answers with the class.

DEFINITION PARAGRAPH

Shinichi Suzuki

[1]Shinichi Suzuki, a Japanese musician who lived from 1898 to 1998, wanted to find a way to teach kids how to play musical instruments. [2]He wanted that method to be easier, more natural, and more effective. [3]He saw how easily and naturally young children learned their first language. [4]He also wondered if children could learn to play musical instruments in the same way. [5]This thinking led to the development of the Suzuki Method. [6]Suzuki first called this method the Mother Tongue Method. [7]Suzuki thought that the earlier a child started to learn to play an instrument, the better. [8]The Suzuki method encourages parents to expose their children to music from birth. [9]It then has them start them in formal instruction at age three or four. [10]In the Suzuki Method, formal instruction does not involve traditional methods. [11]Traditional methods include studying music theory and learning to read music. [12]Students of the Suzuki Method first learn to play an instrument by experimenting on their own and through trial and error. [13]This is what they do when learning their first language.

---

1. Combine sentences 1 and 2 by replacing *He wanted that method to be* with *that was*. This puts the main idea of the paragraph into the first sentence.

2. In sentence 1 change *kids* to a more formal term.

3. In sentence 2, the essential adjective clause *that was easier, more natural, and more effective* does not state what is being compared. Add *than traditional methods*.

4. In sentence 3, find a more academic and specific term for *saw*.

5. Combine sentences 3 and 4 with the conjunction *and* to connect the two ideas which led to Suzuki's method. You do not need to say *he* twice so delete it from sentence 4.

6. Combine sentences 5 and 6 by making sentence 6 into an adjective clause.

7. Combine sentences 8 and 9. Replace *It then has them* with *and then start them* to make the first and second parts of the new sentence parallel.

8. In sentence 10, add *however* after *the Suzuki Method* to show contrast with the previous sentence.

9. Sentence 11 defines *traditional methods*. Combine sentences 10 and 11 by changing sentence 10 into an essential adjective clause. To do this you will need to delete *Traditional methods*.

10. Start sentence 12 with *In contrast* and a comma. Combine sentences 12 and 13 by making sentence 13 into a nonessential adjective clause.

ACTIVITY 12   Original Writing

On a separate sheet of paper, write a definition paragraph (at least six sentences). Explain what the term means. Then give facts, details, and examples. Use at least one example of an essential adjective clause and one example of a nonessential adjective clause.

Here are some examples of how to begin.

- *House music is a type of electronic music that is especially good for dancing.*
- *Sailboarding is a water sport that is easy to learn.*
- *Green gardeners are gardeners who have learned environmental gardening techniques.*

A driver in Hue, Vietnam, checks his cell phone as he pedals tourists in his pedicab.

8 Writing with Adverb Clauses

WHAT DO YOU KNOW?

DISCUSS Look at the photo and read the caption. Discuss the questions.

1. Can people safely use their cell phones while driving? Explain your answer.

2. When do you multitask, or do more than one thing at the same time?

FIND THE ERRORS This paragraph contains two errors with adverb clauses. Find the errors and correct them. Explain your corrections to a partner.

DESCRIPTIVE PARAGRAPH

Multitasking

[1] Can people really multitask, and is it even a good thing to do? [2] Recent research indicates the answer to both those questions could be *no*. [3] According to research, when people multitask, they are not actually focusing on more than one thing at once even though think that they are. [4] Instead, they are moving their attention between the tasks they are doing. [5] Moving their focus between tasks can be very tiring, and this is a problem. [6] Because people are less likely to perform tasks well when they are tired. [7] For these reasons, the next time you try to accomplish more than one challenging task at a time, you might think about just completing one task and then moving on to the next. [8] You might find that you complete both your tasks better and faster that way.

Grammar Forms

8.1 Adverb Clauses

An adverb clause is a kind of dependent clause. It has a subordinating conjunction, a subject, and a verb. It must be joined to an independent clause.

Pattern	Example
1. Adverb clause subordinating conjunction + subject + verb	Many people feel a lot hungrier **when** they do not get enough sleep. SC S V
2. Adverb clauses within sentences **a.** independent clause + adverb clause **b.** adverb clause + comma + independent clause	**a.** There have been fewer accidents on the road since the speed limits were reduced. **b.** Since the speed limits were reduced, there have been fewer accidents on the road.

Notes

1. When the adverb clause is first, a comma separates the clauses.
2. In writing, adverb clauses that begin with *because* or *although* usually go at the beginning of the sentence.
    Although Orcas are called killer whales, they are not a threat to humans in the wild.
3. An adverb clause by itself is an incomplete sentence, or a fragment.
4. Common subordinating conjunctions include *after, although, as soon as, because, before, even though, once, since, so that, though, until, when, whereas, whenever,* and *while.* They are also called connectors.

ACTIVITY 1

Read each sentence. Underline the adverb clauses and label the subordinating conjunctions with *SC* in the sentences. Some of the sentences have more than one adverb clause.

1. Although many children play on sports teams these days, parents should be aware that sports injuries in children can be serious and take a while to heal.

2. The number of cigarette smokers did not decrease until the middle of the twentieth century when people started to become aware of tobacco's health risks.

3. Dermatologists believe that everyone should put sunscreen on their faces to protect their skin whenever they go outside.

4. After cell phone cameras improved, digital camera sales dropped significantly.

5. When people watch a solar eclipse, it is important for them to use special glasses to avoid eye injuries.

6. While fruit is generally considered a healthy snack, eating a lot of fruit can be unhealthy because of the high quantities of fructose in fruit.

7. Although people may feel tired, once they start exercising, they often feel more energized.

8. Because the bark of the giant sequoia tree is so thick, it can survive forest fires and lightning strikes better than many other types of trees.

ACTIVITY 2

Complete the sentences. Use your own ideas. Add a comma when necessary.

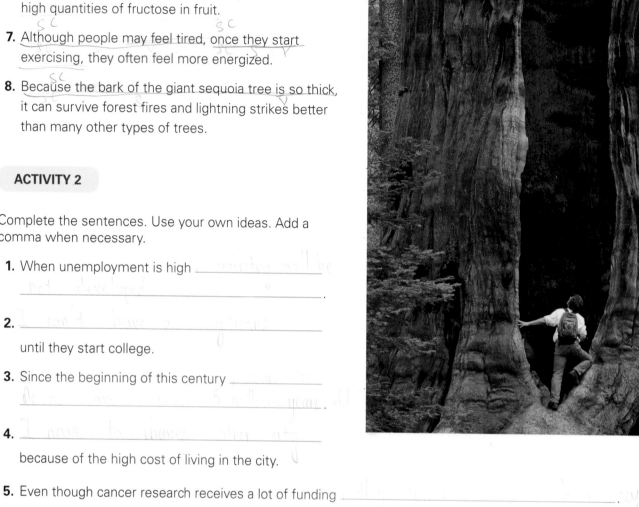

1. When unemployment is high _____ .

2. _____ until they start college.

3. Since the beginning of this century _____ .

4. _____ because of the high cost of living in the city.

5. Even though cancer research receives a lot of funding _____ .

6. _____ so that they have more energy during the day.

Common Uses

8.2 Using Adverb Clauses

Adverb clauses are commonly used in academic writing to express relationships between ideas in a sentence. They often indicate *when, where, how,* or *why* something happened. Adverb clauses are used to express:

1. a reason or cause (with *because, since,* or *as*)	Some people overeat **because** they are depressed.
2. a contrast between ideas (with *while, although, though, even though,* or *whereas*)	**While** it is well-known that musical training develops children's motor skills, recent research shows it also helps children mature emotionally.
3. a concession; an opposing idea that is surprising (with *although, though, even though,* or *while*)	**Although** autism is considered a mental disability, some autistic people are highly skilled in art, music, or math.
4. a purpose (with *so* or *so that*)	Some people move to big cities **so (that)** they do not have to waste time commuting to work.
5. a time relationship (with *after, as soon as, before, when, while, until, whenever, as, once,* or *since*)	Sleep doctors say that it is better for people to go to sleep **as soon as** they feel tired.

ACTIVITY 3

Underline the adverb clause in each sentence. Then write the letter of the purpose of the adverb clause from the box below on the line.

a. a reason or cause	**c.** a concession	**e.** a time relationship
b. a contrast between ideas	**d.** a purpose	

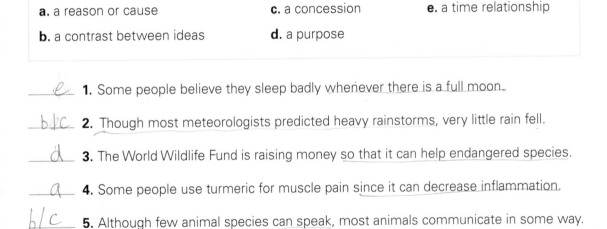

_____*e*____ **1.** Some people believe they sleep badly whenever there is a full moon.

__*b/c*__ **2.** Though most meteorologists predicted heavy rainstorms, very little rain fell.

_____*d*____ **3.** The World Wildlife Fund is raising money so that it can help endangered species.

_____*a*____ **4.** Some people use turmeric for muscle pain since it can decrease inflammation.

__*b/c*__ **5.** Although few animal species can speak, most animals communicate in some way.

Common Errors

Common Error 8.1 Is there a comma missing?

When babies are first born, they cry without shedding tears.

REMEMBER: If the adverb clause begins the sentence, use a comma.

ACTIVITY 4 Common Error 8.1

Some of the following sentences are missing commas. Underline the subordinating conjunctions. Then write *C* if the sentence is correct and *X* if it is missing a comma. Finally, add commas where needed.

_____ 1. Although meditating for 15 minutes or longer is better, even a few minutes of meditation can reduce stress.

___C___ 2. In Nepal, communities are working with wildlife authorities so that they can eliminate the killing of tigers.

_____ 3. Because it has a strict outdoor lighting policy, Flagstaff, Arizona, was declared the first International Dark Sky Community in 2001.

_____ 4. Though many people thought it was too dangerous, Laura Dekker sailed around the world alone at the age of 16.

___C___ 5. In 2012, over 75 percent of the world's population was already using cell phones even though they only came into common use in the late 1990s.

_____ 6. Because the monsoon rains in India started late, farmers are concerned that they may have fewer crops this year.

___C___ 7. In many cultures, parents pick up their babies as soon as they start to cry.

_____ 8. Once the *Titanic* hit the iceberg, it only took two hours and forty minutes to sink.

Common Error 8.2 Is it a fragment?

Although scientists researched the problem for many ~~years. They~~ years, they were not able to find a solution.

REMEMBER: An adverb clause must be joined to an independent clause to form a sentence. An adverb clause that is not joined to an independent clause is an incomplete sentence, or a fragment.

Read the following sentences and underline the subordinating conjunctions. Write *S* if it is a complete sentence. Write *F* if it is a fragment. Be prepared to explain how you would correct the fragment.

_____ **1.** Some people call a doctor whenever they feel sick, while others prefer to wait a day or two.

_____ **2.** Because raccoons have been able to adjust to life in urban centers very well in many parts of the U.S.

_____ **3.** While some people say they never forget a face.

_____ **4.** After there is lightning, there is always thunder.

_____ **5.** Although in the past American young people typically moved out of their parents' homes after they graduated from high school.

_____ **6.** A rooster crows so that other roosters will know to keep away.

_____ **7.** The Sagrada Familia Church in Barcelona still is not finished even though.

_____ **8.** People sweat from certain glands when they get hot and from different glands when they are anxious.

Common Error 8.3   Does each clause have a subject and a verb?

                                                          they
They began planning for the building of the memorial after ⌃ agreed on the design.

                                                    received
Although everyone is familiar with the yellow smiley face, its designer ⌃ only $45.00 for it because he never obtained a patent.

REMEMBER: Both the adverb clause and the independent clause need a subject and verb.

ACTIVITY 6   Common Error 8.3

In each paragraph below, some subjects and verbs are missing from the adverb clauses and independent clauses. Fill in the blanks with the missing words or phrases from the box above the paragraph.

are	has	most people	the empty space is

1.   While the human body _____ several billion atoms, it also contains a vast amount of empty space. In fact, there is so much empty space that once all _____ removed, the remaining atoms _____ no bigger than a sugar cube. Another interesting fact about these atoms is that they are present in everything on the planet. However, there are different types of atoms, although _____ are only familiar with a few of them.

obtain	rubs	the bees	they cannot obtain	they can produce	the pollen

2.   Plants and bees need each other to survive. The bees eat the plant pollen, and the plants need the bees to transfer the pollen from plant to plant. When _____ eat the pollen, _____ coats their bodies and their faces. Then the bees fly to other plants because _____ enough pollen from just one plant. When the bees land on the next flower, the pollen from the other plant _____ onto the new plant. Plants need this new pollen so that _____ new fruit.

is	is not	it	scientists	that is	these problems

3.   Light pollution is a problem because _____ prevents people from seeing the night skies clearly. Although _____ a problem, it _____ the only problem light pollution causes. Light pollution also causes some health problems. For example, light pollution prevents people from creating enough melatonin. While melatonin _____ necessary for healthy sleep cycles, it may also be important for other things. For example, _____ is possible that melatonin helps to strengthen immune systems since _____ have found links between health problems such as obesity, depression, and certain cancers and too much artificial light at night. Although _____ might be a result of unhealthy sleep patterns, scientists are studying melatonin's other effects on the body.

means	noticed	people	this is	were

4.   At one time, millions of years ago, the seven continents _____
all one continent: the continent of Pangea. Although _____
well known now, _____ were not aware of it until 1912 when a
meteorologist _____ that the continents were like pieces of a puzzle.
Alfred Wegener, the meteorologist, named the continent with the Greek word *Pangea* because it
_____ *all lands* in Greek.

Common Error 8.4   Is there an extra connector?

Although many people think dogs and cats do not like each other, ~~but~~ that is not always the case.

REMEMBER: An adverb clause begins with a subordinating conjunction. Do not add an extra
connector to the independent clause.

ACTIVITY 7   Common Error 8.4

Read each sentence. Underline the subordinating conjunctions. Write *C* if the sentence is correct and *X* if
there is an extra subordinating conjunction. Then cross out the extra subordinating conjunction and write
any corrections above it. In some cases, more than one answer may be possible.

_____C_____ **1.** Babies do not develop kneecaps until they are about six months old.

_____ **2.** ~~While~~ Queen Victoria became the queen of an empire consisting of more than 400 million
people when she was only 18 years old.

_____ **3.** ~~Although~~ recent research on teens and video games has concerned many people because it
appears that video games can be addictive for some teens.

_____C_____ **4.** It is important for people to study the geology of other planets so that they can better
understand the history of the solar system.

_____C_____ **5.** Turtles and many other sea animals return to the beach of their birth when it is time for them
to lay their own eggs or give birth to their young.

_____ **6.** Although it may soon be possible to build an emotion detector similar to a lie detector,
~~whereas~~ the question is whether this new technology would be a good thing or not.

_____ **7.** Because the Atacama Desert in Chile is one of the driest places on Earth, ~~so~~ its soil has been
compared to that on Mars.

_____C_____ **8.** When the Museum of Islamic Art in Qatar opened, I. M. Pei, the famous architect who
designed the building, was already 91 years old.

Academic Vocabulary

Words from the Academic Word List (Sublists 4 and 5)

concentration	emerge	hypothesis	investigations	obvious
debate	goals	implications	labels	options

Source: American Word List (Coxhead 2000)

ACTIVITY 8   **Vocabulary in Academic Writing**

Use the academic vocabulary to complete the sentences.

Subject Area	Example from Academic Writing
Health Sciences	**1.** Although it was _____ by the mid-1960s that tobacco smoke could cause cancer, many people had trouble quitting because they were already addicted to smoking.
Political Science	**2.** The U.S. presidential candidates _____ the election issues several times before the people vote.
Education	**3.** Many students do not make career _____ until after they finish their studies.
Environmental Sciences	**4.** Environmentalists are constantly testing the _____ of carbon dioxide in the air because high levels of it can cause climate change.
Economics	**5.** As the population ages, the government needs to plan for the economic _____ of a large number of retired people in society.
Animal Sciences	**6.** Scientists conducted _____ into the habits of desert bats so that they could use the bats to protect plants from plant-eating insects.
Science	**7.** Once scientists decide on a _____ , they design a research study to test whether it is true or false.
Botany	**8.** The Desert Lily is a plant that can live in the desert for many years until there is enough rain for it to _____ from under the ground.
Sociology	**9.** It can be very difficult for people to make decisions when they have a lot of _____
Nutrition	**10.** Since obesity is a serious problem in the United States, the Food and Drug Administration now requires packaged food _____ that make the serving sizes and calories easy to read.

Put It Together

Review Quiz

Multiple Choice Choose the letter of the correct answer.

1. The water temperature in the ocean was approximately four degrees below freezing _____ the *Titanic* sank.

   a. since   **b.** when   **c.** although   **d.** as soon as

2. Orville and Wilbur Wright did not invent the first airplane _____, but they did invent the aircraft controls that made pilots able to operate the airplanes.

   a. as many people think   **b.** since thought   **c.** while people thinking   **d.** because thought

3. The Woodstock music festival in 1969 was a critical moment in musical history _____ the way people thought about music concerts.

   a. so that changed   **b.** although   **c.** while changed   **d.** because it changed

4. The Hoover Dam, which was built in 1935, was the tallest dam in the world for 33 years _____ a taller dam was built in Northern California.

   a. until   **b.** because   **c.** since   **d.** while

5. With more powerful telescopes, scientists can now see about 300 new galaxies that they were previously unable to see _____ they were hidden by the Milky Way.

   a. because as   **b.** as since   **c.** since   **d.** since because

Error Correction One of the five underlined words or phrases is not correct. Find the error and correct it. Be prepared to explain your answer.

6. Neil Armstrong, <u>the first man to walk on the moon</u>, joined NASA immediately <u>after he left</u> the U.S. Navy <u>in</u> 1952 <u>although did not become</u> an astronaut <u>for</u> 10 more years.

7. <u>After</u> 24 years <u>of both</u> women and men advocating for change, <u>in 1893</u>, New Zealand was the first country <u>to change</u> its laws <u>so then</u> women could vote in national elections.

8. <u>According to</u> recent research, <u>when</u> our eyes <u>moved</u> during the REM (rapid eye movement) period of sleep, we <u>see</u> changing images, which might be why <u>our dreams move</u> from place to place.

ACTIVITY 10 Building Greater Sentences

Combine these short sentences into one sentence. You can add new words and move words around, but you should not add or omit any ideas. More than one answer is possible, but all of these sentences require adverb clauses.

1. **a.** Death Valley is the hottest place in North America.
   b. Death Valley is the driest place in North America.
   c. An enormous amount of plant life exists there.
   d. An enormous amount of animal life exists there.

2. **a.** The human body is made up of atoms.
   b. There are several billion atoms.
   c. It also contains a huge amount of empty space.

3. **a.** Martin Luther King, Jr., gave a speech in 1963.
   b. The speech was his famous "I have a dream" speech.
   c. He gave the speech in Washington, D.C.
   e. Approximately 250,000 people were there.

Read the paragraph. Then follow the directions in the 10 steps to edit the information and composition of this paragraph. Write your revised paragraph on a separate sheet of paper. Be careful with capitalization and punctuation. Check your answers with the class.

NARRATIVE PARAGRAPH

Frogtown

[1] Near Los Angeles, there is a small town alongside the Los Angeles River that most people call Frogtown. [2] Frogtown is not its official name, though. [3] There aren't many frogs there now, but at one time there were thousands and thousands of very small, green frogs there. [4] There were so many frogs there that all the streets and yards were covered with them. [5] The streets and yards being covered with frogs lasted until the 1970s. [6] The frogs started disappearing then because suddenly there were lots of large American bullfrogs in the area, and American bullfrogs eat small frogs. [7] At that time, farmers were raising American bullfrogs to sell to restaurants for their frog legs. [8] However, eating frog legs went out of fashion, so the farmers released their bullfrogs into the wilderness. [9] The bullfrogs found their way to the Los Angeles river. [10] Then the bullfrogs found the small green frogs in Frogtown. [11] They ate them. [12] Then there were hardly any frogs left in Frogtown.

1. Combine sentence 1 and 2. Change *Frogtown* in sentence 2 to *even though that* and delete the *though* at the end of sentence 2. Add a comma before *even though* to make this long sentence easier to read.

2. In sentence 3, change *aren't* to avoid contractions.

3. In sentence 3, add *it is called Frogtown because* after *but* to clarify meaning.

4. In sentence 4, add *at times* before *the streets and yards* for accuracy.

5. In sentence 5, change *The streets and yards being covered with frogs* to *This* to better connect the sentences and avoid repetition.

6. Add the adverb phrase *when the frogs started to disappear from Frogtown* to the end of the sentence 5 to draw attention to the next event in the narrative.

7. Add the question *Where did the American bullfrogs come from?* after sentence 6 to better connect the ideas in the paragraph.

8. In sentence 9, change *The bullfrogs* to *Since American bullfrogs need to be near water, they* to add an explanation.

9. Because sentence 11 is very short, combine it with sentence 10 with *and*.

10. Combine your new sentence with sentence 12. Change *then* to *until*.

ACTIVITY 12 **Original Writing**

On a separate sheet of paper, write a narrative paragraph (at least six sentences) about a topic that interests you. Explain what it is and give facts, details, and/or examples. Use at least one adverb clause and underline it; try to use two if possible.

Here are some examples of how to begin.

- *I learned an important lesson when ...*
- *My ideas about . . . changed when I ...*
- *An important event that happened in my hometown was ...*

While teaching in Afghanistan, Masuda Mohamadi wrote detailed e-mails to family and friends in Fairfax, Virginia.

9 Writing with Articles

WHAT DO YOU KNOW?

DISCUSS Look at the photo and read the caption. Discuss the questions.

1. What is your earliest childhood memory?
2. Why do scientists study the brain?

FIND THE ERRORS This paragraph contains two errors with *a*, *an*, or *the*. Find the errors and correct them. Explain your corrections to a partner.

CLASSIFICATION PARAGRAPH

Types of Long-Term Memory

[1] Memory may be classified as short term or long term. [2] Long-term memory is further divided into two categories: explicit and implicit. [3] Explicit memory is used when trying to recall a specific fact or event. [4] Examples of explicit memory include remembering dates and historical events in order to answer a question on exam or recalling when a recent purchase was made. [5] In contrast, implicit memory, often referred to as procedural memory, is automatic. [6] Procedural memory develops from repetition: performing the same action over and over again. [7] Over time, the action becomes "automatic," and a person no longer has to think about the steps to perform it. [8] Examples of procedural memory include riding a bicycle, formatting a computer document, and brushing one's teeth. [9] Explicit and implicit, or procedural, memories are stored in different areas of brain.

Grammar Forms

9.1   Articles

Indefinite articles

The indefinite articles *a / an* come before singular count nouns and noun phrases.

a + (consonant sound)	**A** survey is commonly used to collect data for research.
	A college may offer two- or four-year degrees, while **a** university also offers postgraduate degrees.
an + (vowel sound)	**An** open-ended question on a survey allows the participant to express **an** opinion or feeling.
	An anthropology course might have **an** enrollment of 35 students, whereas **an** honors course in anthropology might have only 15 students.

Definite article

The definite article *the* comes before specific nouns. They can be singular or plural.

the	**The** survey asked 100 college students to rate their professors.
	The courses that college students take in their first year vary according to their major.

No article (Ø)

No article is used before plural nouns when referring to general categories. In addition, no article is used before abstract nouns and general noncount nouns.

No article (Ø)	**Surveys** are useful for obtaining feedback from customers.
	(*surveys* = plural noun)
	Psychology is one of the most popular college majors today.
	(*psychology* = abstract noun)

Read the following sentences. Underline the nouns and noun phrases and identify the type of article that comes before them. Then write the total number of each article in the boxes. The first one is done for you.

	a	an	the	no article
1. An example of a pack animal is the South American llama.	1	1	1	0
2. After residents saw an increase in crime, they established a neighborhood watch program.				
3. An individual entering the workforce needs to take responsibility for personal and professional decisions.				
4. A hypothesis is a prediction and is based on a theory that a researcher can test.				
5. In the experiment, the participants made a commitment to provide accurate answers to the questions on the survey.				
6. A common mistake for first-time homebuyers is forgetting to include the cost of property taxes and insurance in their budget.				
7. Global warming is a universal issue that concerns most of the countries around the world.				
8. A professional relationship with a mentor is one way to develop leadership skills and career opportunities.				
9. The low number of respondents to the survey was a huge disappointment to the researchers.				
10. In an effort to protect endangered African elephants, the United States has enforced a strict ban on commercial imports of ivory.				

Common Uses

9.2 Using Indefinite Articles

The indefinite articles *a* and *an* occur before singular count nouns. Use them:

1. to introduce something for the first time	**A** law to protect endangered species was passed in 1973. The law protected both plants and animals.
2. to define or classify something	**An** artery is a blood vessel that carries blood away from the heart.
3. to refer to one member of a group • The statement is true of all members of the group.	The fur of **a** polar bear is thicker than any other bear's fur.

9.3 Using the Definite Article

The definite article *the* occurs before singular and plural count nouns and with noncount nouns. Use it:

1. to refer to something that is unique	During a solar eclipse, **the** sky becomes so dark that some stars become visible.
2. to refer to something introduced earlier	A law to protect endangered species was passed in 1973. **The** law protected both plants and animals.
3. to refer to knowledge that is familiar to or shared by the reader	Most people are opposed to **the** new tax law.
4. to refer to the members of a group or to the entire class or category • The statement is true of all members of the group.	**The** giant panda is endangered despite efforts to preserve its natural habitat.
5. to refer to a specific person or thing • The person or thing is often identified in a prepositional phrase or adjective clause.	**The** money for the class trip to the nation's capital was raised by several charities. **The** athlete that fans respected most was modest about his accomplishments.
6. to show rankings, especially with superlatives	**The** best way to prevent heart disease is through a good diet and physical exercise.

9.3 Using the Definite Article (continued)

Notes

1. Use the definite article *the* with quantity phrases such as *all of*, *most of*, *some of*, and *none of*.

   Most of **the** participants in the study felt they benefited from one-on-one tutoring.

2. The definite article is sometimes used to refer to geographical names. For more information, see Appendix 3, Capitalization and Punctuation, page 218.

   The United States is home to **the** Mississippi River, the third longest river in North America.

3. The definite article is used with a singular noun to make a general statement, especially in technical and scientific writing.

   The computer has influenced the way people communicate in several ways.

9.4 Using No Article (Ø)

Sometimes no article occurs before a noun. Do not use an article:

1. to refer to general categories or groups	**Polar bears** cannot live on land due to their inability to dig with their paws.
2. to make a general statement with a noncount noun	**Pollution** is one of the most pressing environmental problems countries face today.
3. to make a general statement with a plural noun	**Studies** show that many consumers are not saving enough for their retirement.
4. to refer to some diseases or illnesses: *arthritis, cancer, AIDS, polio, heart disease, diabetes, high blood pressure*	The number of people suffering from **diabetes** is expected to increase sharply over the next two to three decades.

Notes

1. An article is not used to refer to proper nouns: specific places, people, businesses, and publications.

   Sam Walton founded both **Sam's Club** and **Walmart**.

2. An article is generally not used to refer to days, months, seasons, and holidays.

   December 21, the first day of **winter**, has a long history of celebrations dating back to Stonehenge.

   An exception is that *the* can be used to refer to a specific season in a specific place.

   The winters in Saskatchewan are much colder than **the winters** in Florida.

Fill in the blanks with *a, an, the,* or Ø (no article). If an article begins a sentence, capitalize it and change the capital letter of the next word to lowercase.

1. _____ Growing season in _____ United States varies according to the region of the country. It is shorter in _____ Alaska and longer in _____ Florida, for example.

2. _____ Students who major in _____ education often take _____ course in how to create _____ atmosphere of positive learning.

3. _____ Vaccines are available for the prevention of a number of diseases including _____ smallpox, _____ polio, and _____ tuberculosis.

4. People who dislike reading _____ fiction may find _____ narrative non-fiction, which tells _____ story but is based on fact, more enjoyable.

5. _____ Unsafe product on store shelves puts all _____ consumers at risk.

6. _____ Alphanumeric password contains _____ letters, _____ numbers, and/or _____ symbols and is _____ best choice for protecting one's personal information.

7. _____ Internet is _____ group of networks that allows users to access _____ information and to communicate with others around _____ world.

8. _____ Recently published study indicates that _____ person's taste in music may offer insight into his or her personality.

9. _____ Astrophysicists have _____ different opinions on how _____ galaxy that we live in, _____ Milky Way, was formed.

10. Working as _____ research assistant at _____ university often involves collecting and putting _____ data into _____ spreadsheet.

Common Errors

Common Errors

Common Error 9.1   Is the article *a* or *an* missing?

In some cultures, it is uncommon for *a* man to shake hands with *a* woman.

In 1964, the Beatles introduced *a* new type of music to listeners in the United States.

An analogy
~~Analogy~~ is the comparison of an unfamiliar item to a familiar one.

REMEMBER: Use *a* or *an* with singular count nouns.

✓ **ACTIVITY 3**   **Common Error 9.1**

Add the missing articles *a* or *an* in the correct locations. Change capitalization as needed. The number of missing articles is in parentheses.

1. Taking short quiz is effective way to prepare for exam. (3)

2. Psychology is science. It is the scientific study of mental processes and human behavior. (1)

3. Paralegal assists lawyer with tasks such as conducting research, organizing files, and preparing for meetings, trials, and hearings. (2)

4. Andrew Carnegie, leader in the U.S. steel industry in the late nineteenth century, said, "When fate hands us lemon, let's try to make lemonade." (2)

5. Lionfish is invasive fish that poses threat to humans and other fish in the waters off the United States. (3)

6. "The Interlopers" is short story by H. H. Munro, who wrote under the name of Saki. The story is about two men who are involved in longtime family disagreement. (2)

7. Professional dancer is athlete, someone who trains every day to perfect his or her performance. (2)

8. Fossil fuels, such as oil, natural gas, or coal, are nonrenewable energy source. (1)

Common Error 9.2 Is the article *the* missing?

          the
Prospective candidates for job made presentations to the committee.

The body's
~~Body's~~ circulatory system is extremely long, longer than the circumference of the earth.

    the
Many of international students who are denied visas later reapply.

REMEMBER: Use *the* when referencing a noun that is specific, familiar to the reader, or after a quantity expression.

ACTIVITY 4   Common Error 9.2

Add the missing article *the* in the correct locations. Change capitalization as needed. The number of missing articles is in parentheses.

1. One of best ways to learn a second language is to live in a country where people speak language. (2)

2. People living along Atlantic coast may someday have to move inland due to rising sea levels. (1)

3. Spanish explorers brought horse to New World, an animal that proved useful for the Native Americans living there. (2)

4. Steve Jobs introduced iPhone to world in 2007, and Apple has sold close to one billion units. (2)

5. Many of organic fruits and vegetables consumers buy are from farmers who live in local community. (2)

6. During spring and autumnal equinoxes, sun passes directly over the equator. (2)

7. The American white ibis, a tropical bird with white feathers and a long, curved, red-orange bill, lives along southern coastline of United States. (2)

Common Error 9.3   Are you making a general or specific reference?

            an   The
The senator proposed ~~the~~ addition to the new bill. ~~An~~ addition would allocate educational funds for women entering the field of engineering.

           a   a   a
Many people who own ~~the~~ smartphone prefer to send ~~the~~ text rather than to make ~~the~~ call.

REMEMBER: Use the definite article *the* when making a specific reference to something and the indefinite article *a* or *an* to make a general one.

Underline the correct articles.

1. (*An* / *The*) explorer Christopher Columbus introduced (*a* / *the*) lemon to Haiti.

2. Taking public transportation benefits both people and (*the* / *an*) environment by reducing (*the* / *a*) number of cars on the road.

3. There are several reasons almost every college student owns (*the* / *a*) computer.

4. Obtaining (*a* / *the*) college degree has (*the* / *a*) positive effect on (*the* / *a*) amount of one's lifetime earnings. (*An* / *The*) difference over a lifetime can be as much as $400,000.

5. (*The* / *A*) beaker is (*the* / *a*) glass container that is used in (*the* / *a*) chemistry lab.

6. Mahatma Gandhi led (*a* / *the*) model life as (*an* / *the*) activist for nonviolence.

7. Charles Lindbergh, famous for his nonstop flight from New York to Paris, was (*the* / *a*) graduate of (*a* / *the*) University of Wisconsin–Madison.

8. Building inspectors use (*a* / *the*) term *egress* to refer to the ways (*the* / *a*) person can exit a building: doors, windows, and hallways, for example.

9. (*A* / *The*) United States is (*an* / *the*) example of (*a* / *the*) democracy.

10. Antonie van Leeuwenhoek of (*a* / *the*) Netherlands was (*a* / *the*) first person to see (*a* / *the*) living cell with (*a* / *the*) microscope.

Common Error 9.4   Is an article used where one is not needed?

Computers, printers, and office furniture are examples of items listed as ~~an~~ equipment in a company's budget.

Today, ~~the~~ online classes are growing in popularity as they allow students the flexibility to study at the time and place they choose.

A group of experts believes that over the next ten years, identifying who is at risk for ~~the~~ cancer will lead to a cure for the disease.

REMEMBER: • Do not use *a* or *an* with noncount nouns.
• Do not use *the* with plural nouns when referring to general categories.
• Do not use an article with specific diseases.

In each sentence, cross out the articles that are not needed. The number of articles not needed is in parentheses.

1. When the college students need the career advice, they can visit the career center on their campus or meet with an advisor. (2)

2. Studies show that the teenagers are heavily influenced by the actions of their peers. (1)

3. As a result of the technology, a communication between the people has changed in numerous ways. (3)

4. The use of the technology in the classroom has both the positive and negative effects on an education. (3)

5. Research suggests that working on a team enhances the creativity, improves the communication, and results in a shared learning. (3)

6. A recent poll shows that many people believe that reading the e-books has several disadvantages over reading the print books. (2)

7. For the immigrants, adjusting to a new culture often causes the anxiety and may even lead to the depression. (3)

8. Creating the art has a number of benefits: it relieves the stress and increases brain function. (2)

Academic Vocabulary

Nouns Frequently Used in Academic Writing

education	health	number	research	studies
example	increase	participants	result	variety

Source: Corpus of Contemporary American English (Davies 2008–)

ACTIVITY 7 **Vocabulary in Academic Writing**

Use the academic vocabulary to complete the sentences. Use *a, an,* or *the* when needed. For some sentences, more than one answer is possible.

Subject Area	Example from Academic Writing
Education	1. _____ shows that the sooner children learn to read, the better they will do in school.
History	2. In November of 1989, the Berlin wall came down; as _____, East and West Germany reunited a year later.
Psychology	3. _____ of a common behavioral disorder in teens is social anxiety, a symptom of which is feeling self-conscious around others.
Art	4. In a recent study, _____ who completed a six-week art appreciation course stated that they had gained a better understanding of other cultures and societies.
Business	5. The small-business owner can choose from _____ of loan options in order to establish or grow a business.
Political Science	6. _____ of registered voters who go to the polls on election day increases when voters believe they have the power to change things.
Literature	7. Literature has an important role in _____: to stimulate students' reading, thinking, discussion, and analytical skills.
Environmental Science	8. Recent _____ in environmental science have examined the effect of pollution on children's ability to control their behavior.
Health	9. _____ in the amount of fruit and vegetables in one's daily diet can decrease the risk of heart disease and stroke.
Computer Science	10. A group of computer scientists has developed an app to collect data as a way to assess _____ of smartphone users, including whether they suffer from depression.

Put It Together

ACTIVITY 8   Review Quiz

Multiple Choice Choose the letter of the correct answer.

1. Birds are endotherms, which means they are _____ animals that have a stable body temperature.

   a. a   **b.** an   **c.** (no article)   **d.** the

2. In literature, _____ main character usually struggles with an inner conflict, such as fear of change.

   a. a   **b.** an   **c.** (no article)   **d.** the

3. Becoming a registered nurse (RN) requires _____ Associate of Science degree in Nursing, which may take from two to three years to obtain.

   a. a   **b.** an   **c.** (no article)   **d.** the

4. The Internet is a good resource for tips on how to market a product to _____ potential customers.

   a. a   **b.** an   **c.** (no article)   **d.** the

5. Students should consider taking a physical education course in college because of _____ health benefits it provides.

   a. a   **b.** an   **c.** (no article)   **d.** the

Error Correction One of the five underlined words or phrases is not correct. Find the error and correct it. Be prepared to explain your answer.

6. Recent <u>studies</u> show <u>a growing demand</u> for <u>retirement communities</u> that offer

   residents safe and comfortable living space, <u>the access</u> to medical care, and

   <u>a full calendar</u> of social activities.

7. When writing <u>academic essays</u>, <u>writers</u> should avoid making <u>hasty generalizations</u>

   and <u>exaggerated claims</u> in order to avoid offending <u>an audience</u> they are trying to

   reach.

8. <u>People</u> who buy <u>the bottled water</u> often think they are helping <u>the environment</u>

   when, in fact, they are contributing to <u>pollution</u> by using <u>plastic bottles</u>.

Visitors view the lower falls from a footbridge at Multnomah Falls.

Building Greater Sentences

Combine these short sentences into one sentence. You can add new words and move words around, but you should not add or omit any ideas. More than one answer is possible, but all of these sentences require definite and/or indefinite articles.

1. a. The Columbia River Gorge is home to Multnomah Falls.

   b. Multnomah Falls is the tallest waterfall in Oregon.

   c. Multnomah Falls has a height of 620 feet.

_____

_____

2. a. The U.S. government encouraged people to plant "victory gardens."

   b. Victory gardens made more fresh food available.

   c. Victory gardens allowed citizens to show their patriotism for the country.

   d. This happened during World War II.

_____

_____

3. a. A child who plays sports may have better grades than a child who does not play sports.

   b. The child may also develop stronger relationships with his or her peers.

   c. The child may exhibit more self-confidence.

   d. Studies show this is true.

_____

_____

Steps to Composing

Read the paragraph. Then follow the directions in the 10 steps to edit the information and composition of this paragraph. Write your revised paragraph on a separate sheet of paper. Be careful with capitalization and punctuation. Check your answers with the class.

CAUSE-EFFECT

Becoming an Everyday Environmentalist

[1] People can take some steps to protect the environment. [2] One of the easiest steps is turning off the lights when leaving a room. [3] Turning off the lights saves electricity and lowers one's electric bill. [4] One more step is to turn on a fan and raise the setting on the air conditioner. [5] This will make the people in the room feel cooler. [6] In addition to conserving energy, people can also take steps to conserve water. [7] One way is to shut off the water while brushing their teeth. [8] This behavior saves water as well as money. [9] Another way to save money is to get tap water instead of buying water in a bottle. [10] Bottled water is more expensive than tap water, and it comes in plastic bottles, which contribute to pollution. [11] People can plant gardens. [12] Growing vegetables at home helps the environment by enriching the soil as well as providing organic produce at a much lower cost than buying produce at a supermarket. [13] There are numerous ways people can help save the environment, and these first steps are both easy and rewarding.

---

1. In sentence 1, the word *some* is vague. Change it to the more specific phrase *several simple*.

2. In sentence 3, the introductory phrase *Turning off the lights* is repetitive. Change it to *this step*.

3. In sentence 4, *one more* is informal. Replace it with *another*.

4. In sentence 5, replace *This* with *The fan* to create a smooth transition between sentences 4 and 5.

5. In sentence 9, the verb *get* is vague and informal. Change it to *drink*.

6. In sentence 9, change *water in a bottle* to *bottled water*.

7. In sentence 10, delete *it comes in*, the comma, and *which*. This will clearly show that plastic bottles (not water) cause pollution

8. In sentence 11, introduce the last step with *Finally* and a comma.

9. In sentence 12, the phrase *helps the environment by enriching the soil as well as providing* is wordy. Shorten it to *enriches the soil and provides*.

10. In sentence 12, *buying* is informal. Change it to the more academic word *purchasing*.

ACTIVITY 11   **Original Writing**

On a separate sheet of paper, write a cause-effect paragraph (at least six sentences). Explain either the causes or the effects of an action or event. Use indefinite and definite articles in your paragraph.

Here are some examples of how to begin.

- *There are several ways to learn a foreign language more quickly.*
- *Taking a weekly one-day break from all technology will result in several key personal benefits.*
- *Three reasons people gain weight are lack of exercise, unhealthy diet, and insufficient sleep.*

Employees rest at Dunas Stadium during preparation for the 2014 FIFA World Cup in Natal, Brazil.

10 Writing Simple and Compound Sentences

WHAT DO YOU KNOW?

DISCUSS Look at the photo and read the caption. Discuss the questions.

1. Do you think napping during the day is a good or bad idea? Explain.

2. Do you (or does anyone you know) have trouble sleeping at night? How can people sleep better?

FIND THE ERRORS This paragraph contains two errors. Find the errors and correct them. Explain your corrections to a partner.

PROBLEM-SOLUTION PARAGRAPH

Sleeping Cold

[1] Many people have problems getting enough sleep. [2] For some, it is a problem of going to sleep late at night and having to get up early in the morning. [3] For others the problem is either having trouble falling asleep, or not being able to stay asleep. [4] The Internet is full of solutions to try from drinking chamomile tea to not using electronic screens before going to bed. [5] However, may be an easier way to get more sleep. [6] Recent studies show some people have trouble sleeping because their bedrooms are too warm. [7] This is because falling body temperatures make people drowsy, but rising body temperatures wake people up. [8] According to these studies, the ideal temperature for sleeping is between 60 and 67 degrees Fahrenheit (or 16 and 19 degrees Celsius), it might be worth turning down the thermostat in your house, or opening a window before going to sleep.

Grammar Forms

10.1 Simple Sentences

A simple sentence contains only one independent clause. That independent clause must express a complete idea and have at least one subject and one verb.

Independent clauses

1 subject + 1 verb	A stalk of celery contains only about 10 calories. 　　　　　　S　　　　　　　V
1 subject + 2 or more verbs	Celery helps the stomach digest food and reduces blood pressure. 　S　　V　　　　　　　　　　　　　　　　　V
2 or more subjects + 1 verb	Celery and kale reduce blood pressure. 　S　　　　S　　　V Celery, kale, and other leafy greens reduce blood pressure. 　S　　　S　　　　　　　S　　　　　V
Imperative form of verb	Notice the difference in color in the two liquids. 　V

Notes

1. A simple sentence has only one clause, which means one subject–verb combination. A simple sentence can have two subjects or two verbs, but there is only one subject–verb relationship.

2. Use a comma between three or more items in a series. Do not use a comma between two items.

    Japan, China, and Cambodia import oil.

    Japan and China import oil.

3. The basic word order of simple sentences is one of the four below:

    a. S + V + direct object (for action verbs with direct objects)

        Many children do not eat celery very often.

    b. S + V (+ prepositional phrase) (for nonaction verbs that do not take direct objects)

        William Shakespeare died in 1616.

    c. S + *be* + adjective/noun phrase

        Vegetables are nutritious.

    d. S + V + noun phrase

        Curing the common cold is still a challenge for scientists.

4. Prepositional phrases can be added to basic sentence patterns. When a prepositional phrase is at the beginning of a sentence, use a comma.

    There are 12 months in the solar calendar.

    In the solar calendar, there are 12 months.

A compound sentence has two or more independent clauses that are connected by a coordinating conjunction. Three common coordinating conjunctions in academic writing are *and, but,* and *so.*

Coordinating Conjunctions

and	The moon is a satellite of the earth, **and** it circles around the sun.
but	The first manned landing on the moon was in 1969, **but** the first unmanned one was in 1959.
so	Gravity is weaker on the moon, **so** everything on the moon weighs less.

Notes

1. A comma is used before the coordinating conjunction in a compound sentence.

   Both temperate and tropical rainforests have high amounts of rainfall, but the average temperature in tropical rainforests is higher.

2. Academic sentences do not usually begin with conjunctions.

ACTIVITY 1

Underline the subject(s) in each sentence. Label each verb with *V.* Then write the kind of sentence on the line: *S* (simple sentence) or *C* (compound sentence).

S **1.** Most wild animals depend on their instincts more than on learned behavior.

C **2.** Fantasy and science-fiction movies help people escape from the world around them, but documentaries make people think about the world around them.

C **3.** Maple trees and oak trees are both deciduous trees, so they lose their leaves in the winter.

C **4.** High quality dark chocolate contains iron and other nutrients, but it is very high in calories and fat.

S **5.** Schools develop children's minds and improve their social skills.

S **6.** Hawaii, Italy, Reunion Island, and the Democratic Republic of the Congo have the most active volcanoes in the world.

C **7.** People used to get the news mainly from the radio, TV, or newspapers, but these days many people find out about the news from social media and Internet sites.

S **8.** According to the most recent reports, self-driving cars should make people's lives easier and the roads safer.

Common Uses

10.3 Using Simple Sentences

Simple sentences are used in academic writing to focus the readers' attention on one piece of information. They are used:

1. to state information • In academic writing, this is the most common use.	The most recently discovered metal, ununseptium, is now the heaviest metal on the periodic table.
2. to give instructions or make a request • This directs the reader's attention to something specific or new.	Note the population changes of the world's largest cities over the last decade. Let us now investigate the recent activity in the San Andreas Fault on the Pacific Coast.
3. to ask a question • This may be used in an introduction (as a hook to get the reader's attention) or in a concluding sentence.	How does the brain process language? How will speech therapists use this information on brain processing to help their patients?
4. to express strong emotion or an opinion • This often occurs in persuasive writing.	People should not be allowed to smoke in public places.

10.4 Using Compound Sentences

Compound sentences are used in academic writing to connect related ideas. The coordinating conjunction shows the relationship between ideas. Coordinating conjunctions are used:

1. to add information about a topic or compare two topics (with *and*)	Kitchen fires are the most common cause of house fires, **and** faulty heating systems are the second most common cause.
2. to show contrasting information about a topic (with *but*)	Brazil has the largest population in South America, **but** Ecuador has the greatest population density.
3. to show a causal relationship (with the effect in the second clause after *so* (*that*))	In 2016, Mars's orbit was closer to Earth's orbit than usual, **so** many people were able to observe Mars without a telescope.

Notes

1. The three most common conjunctions in academic writing are *and, but,* and *so.* The conjunctions *or, nor, for* and *yet* are not as common in academic writing.

2. Do not use a comma before *so* (*that*) when it introduces a purpose. With a purpose, *so* (*that*) means *in order that*.
   Scientists need to conduct research **so** (that) they can determine the effectiveness of a new medicine.

3. Good academic writing generally includes a variety of simple and compound sentences in the same paragraph.

Read each sentence. Write the purpose of the simple sentences on the line: *I* (giving information), *R* (making a request), *Q* (asking a question), or *O* (expressing an opinion).

_O_ **1.** Food manufacturers should be required to label foods that have genetically modified organisms (GMOs).

_Q_ **2.** Would politicians be more careful about what they said in debates if fact checkers were present?

_R_ **3.** Refer to Figure 4.2 to compare the life spans of termites and cockroaches.

_I_ **4.** Uber and Airbnb both operate in many different countries all over the world.

_I_ **5.** Chart 4.7 shows the average weights and lengths of different kinds of sharks.

_Q_ **6.** Should warning labels have appeared on cigarette packages sooner?

Complete the compound sentences with *and, or, so, but*

1. The musician Prince wrote many different types of songs, _____so_____ he was popular with people from different generations.

2. Studies of infants' brains shows us how infants learn language, _____and_____ they also show that the brain processes music in the same way.

3. Some medications that elderly people take cause them to lose their appetites, _____so_____ they may not eat enough to get the nutrition they need.

4. No one thinks of mirrors as high-tech inventions, _____but_____ how many people can explain how mirrors work?

5. Both manatees and dolphins live in the warm Florida waters, _____but_____ manatees are more sensitive than dolphins to the colder winter water temperatures.

6. TV advertisements have become more creative over the years, _____and_____ some of the best ads can be more entertaining than the TV shows.

7. The cost of solar panels has decreased over the years, _____so_____ more people can afford to buy them for their homes and businesses.

8. Babies learn words with repeated syllables better than words without repeated syllables, _____so_____ expressions like "good night" become "night night."

Common Errors

Common Error 10.1   Does the independent clause have a subject and a verb?

         is
Cinco de Mayo ∧ a holiday to celebrate Mexico's victory over the French in 1862.

                                                it
Despite being a minor holiday in Mexico, in the United States ∧ is celebrated widely with musical performances, parades, and parties.

REMEMBER: All independent clauses must have a subject and a complete verb. The exception is imperative sentences, as the subject (*you*) is understood.

ACTIVITY 4   Common Error 10.1

The sentences below are missing the subjects and verbs in parentheses. Write the missing words in the correct positions. Make all necessary changes in capitalization.

1. Although the southern U.S. states *are* famous for their peach trees, most species need about one month of cooler temperatures, so *they* do not grow well in places that do not have enough cold winter days. (*are; they*)

2. There *is* no limit to the energy we can get from the sun, but only approximately *comes* one percent of the electricity that is used in the world from this source. (*is; comes*)

3. Bats are blind, so *they use* their heightened sense of hearing and echolocation to help them navigate the world. (*they; use*)

4. Up to 65 percent of young children *have* imaginary friends, but not many of those children *will* remember them when they are adults. (*have; will*)

5. The hippocampus is the control center of the memory part of the brain. *It stores* Stores new memories, and it *is* also the part of the brain that retrieves those memories. (*it; is*)

6. Before 1965, most of the in the United States was American, but the "British Invasion" *pop music took over* the American pop music scene in 1965. (*pop music; took over*)

7. According to recent research, *there* is a genetic mutation that allows some people to see more shades of colors than most people can see, and it *seems* only to affect women. (*there; seems*)

8. Captain Cook and his men welcomed by the islanders when they *were* first arrived in Hawaii, but this *was* because the Hawaiians at first thought that they were gods. (*were; was*)

Common Error 10.2　Is a comma missing?

In many societies, it is acceptable for little girls to cry ∧ but it is less acceptable for boys of the
same age to cry.

REMEMBER: In compound sentences, commas are used before coordinating conjunctions that connect two independent clauses.

ACTIVITY 5　**Common Error 10.2**

Add the missing commas.

1. The flood caused extensive damage, but almost every home was later rebuilt.

2. It is difficult to focus well when multitasking, so multitasking while studying is not a good idea.

3. In the 1600s, England, France, and Spain all tried to gain control of the North American continent and there were many conflicts.

4. Environmental engineers work on pollution and energy use, and they also try to solve water, land, and waste issues.

5. Volcanic lightning is very unpredictable and very different from thunderstorm lightning, so scientists still aren't sure what causes it.

6. People are 30 times more likely to be hit by lightning than to be bitten by a shark, but sharks are a lot more frightening to most people.

Common Error 10.3　Is a coordinating conjunction missing?

　　　　　　　　　　　　　　　　　　　　　　　　　　　　　　but
Mixed-use neighborhoods are places where people can work, live, shop, and play in the same
area, ∧ some mixed-use neighborhoods have few job options.
　　　　　　　　　　　　　　　　　bicycle, but
People enjoy commuting by ~~bicycle. But~~ the city needs more bike lanes.

REMEMBER: • Coordinating conjunctions are used to connect independent clauses in one sentence.
　　　　　　　• Coordinating conjunctions are not used at the beginning of a sentence.

ACTIVITY 6   Common Error 10.3

Correct or insert coordinating conjunctions. The number of errors is in parentheses. Add commas where necessary.

1. More and more people are suffering from allergies. These days, nutritionists are recommending that they eat more foods that are high in vitamins C, D, and E. These particular vitamins help to strengthen the immune system, and they can also help to make sneezing, coughing, and itchy eyes less serious. There are also medications that help reduce allergy symptoms, but these medications tend to make people feel drowsy. (3)

2. Almost all birds find mates, and they stay with them for life. This sounds very romantic, but birds probably do not stay with their mates because they are in love. Zoologists believe birds such as geese stay together because it is easier to survive. Instead of spending time fighting with other birds, they can spend that time taking care of their young. It is a very dangerous world for baby birds, so having two parents taking care of the babies means they are more likely to survive. (3)

3. Machu Picchu is an ancient Inca city in Peru that was made a UNESCO World Heritage site in 1983. Most archeologists believe that the Incas built Machu Picchu as a place for an Incan emperor in the fifteenth century, but no one is absolutely certain. It is on a flat area on the top of a 7,970-foot mountain, and it was very difficult to get to. When the Spanish came to colonize Peru in the sisteenth century, the Incas abandoned Machu Picchu. The Spanish destroyed many other beautiful sites, but because they never found Machu Picchu, Machu Picchu was left untouched. Machu Picchu remained untouched until 1911 when an American historian "discovered" it. (4)

4. Lighthouses keep ships from crashing into rocks, and they help to guide ships through dangerous waters or into harbors. They are usually in remote locations far away from cities where there are not many lights at night. They are also near harbors to show ship captains how to get into the harbors. Traditionally, lighthouses have been very tall, narrow, circular towers with a revolving light on the top. In the past, people needed to live in the lighthouses to turn the lights on and to check that everything was working correctly. Now everything is automated, so it is not necessary for people to live in lighthouses anymore. (3)

Academic Vocabulary

Words from the Academic Word List (Sublists 5 and 6)

aware	decline	fundamental	notion	version
capacity	equivalent	generation	ratio	whereas

Source: Academic Word List (Coxhead 2000)

ACTIVITY 7   **Vocabulary in Academic Writing**

Use the academic vocabulary to complete the sentences. For some sentences, more than one answer is possible.

Subject Area	Example from Academic Writing
Philosophy	**1.** Studies show that philosophy classes help many students become more _____ of how they think, and in some cases they can alter the way they view the world and solve problems.
Education	**2.** Students who fail repeatedly in elementary and secondary school often have the _____ that they cannot learn.
Political Science	**3.** Good politicians need the _____ to connect with their voters, but they also need a personality that inspires trust and confidence.
Economics	**4.** Droughts can cause a _____ in fruit and vegetable harvests, so these foods may become more expensive.
Health Sciences	**5.** Recent research shows that both walking and running may provide _____ health benefits as far as heart disease is concerned.
Linguistics	**6.** Most Scandinavian, Latvian, and Dutch people speak more than one language, _____ most British, Italian, and Portuguese people speak only one.
History	**7.** British children learn a very different _____ of what Americans call the Revolutionary War from what American children learn.
Medicine	**8.** Officials are concerned about the low _____ of physicians to residents in urban areas, so they are taking steps to attract more physicians.
Sociology	**9.** The term millennials refers to the _____ of people born after 1980 but before the mid-1990s.
Animal Science	**10.** Scientists used to claim that a _____ difference between animals and humans was that humans have the ability to use tools and animals do not, but now most people recognize that this is not true.

Put It Together

ACTIVITY 8   **Review Quiz**

Multiple Choice   Choose the letter of the correct answer.

1. Plants use sunlight to get all the energy that they need, _____ animals get their energy from eating plants.

   a. so   **b.** or   **c.** and   **d.** for

2. Scientists used to think that Neanderthals were not very intelligent, _____ recent research shows that they used tools, controlled fire, buried their dead, and even cooked vegetables as well as meat.

   a. and   **b.** but   **c.** so   **d.** for

3. Abraham Lincoln did not enter the Civil War to end slavery, _____ did not take him long to realize the importance of ending slavery.

   a. but it   **b.** so he   **c.** and it   **d.** so there

4. Vegetable and animal protein helps the body to feel full longer, _____ protein could help people lose weight.

   a. so eat   **b.** so eating   **c.** but eat   **d.** and eat

5. Astronomers have discovered more than 1,700 planets in our galaxy, _____ are probably many others out there waiting to be discovered.

   a. so there   **b.** but there   **c.** so   **d.** but

Error Correction   One of the five underlined words or phrases is not correct. Find the error and correct it. Be prepared to explain your answer.

6. Urban trees <u>can save</u> cities money <u>by helping</u> with <u>soil erosion energy consumption</u>, and storm water

   erosion, <u>so</u> some cities have hired urban tree specialists to guide <u>them</u> in their efforts to preserve trees.

7. Bette Nesmith Graham, a painter <u>and</u> a typist <u>in the 1950s and 1960s,</u> <u>were</u> frustrated by all the

   mistakes she <u>was making</u> on her electric typewriter, <u>so</u> she created Liquid Paper.

8. In a recent study on friendship, <u>only</u> about <u>50 percent of the</u> acquaintances that people listed as their

   friends actually considered <u>themselves</u> friends, <u>but</u> people <u>are not</u> always the best judges of friendship.

Building Greater Sentences

Combine these short sentences into one sentence. You can add new words and move words around, but you should not add or omit any ideas. More than one answer is possible. These sentences require compound sentences and the addition of *and, but,* or *so.*

1. a. Human babies are born very helpless.
   b. Human babies are more helpless than other animal newborns.
   c. Human babies need to stay with their parents.
   d. Human babies stay with their parents for a very long time.

_____

_____

2. a. There has been a lot of research on mindfulness training.
   b. Research shows that mindfulness training can improve people's physical and mental health.
   c. No one is sure how or why mindfulness training helps.

_____

_____

3. a. Scientists are using the laws of math to estimate things.
   b. Scientists estimate how many living species are on the earth.
   c. Scientists estimate that there may be about one trillion.

_____

_____

Read the paragraph. Then follow the directions in the 10 steps to edit the information and composition of this paragraph. Write your revised paragraph on a separate sheet of paper. Be careful with capitalization and punctuation. Check your answers with the class.

COMPARISON PARAGRAPH

Cultural Interpretations of Facial Expressions

[1] Facial expressions may be similar all over the world. [2] The way facial expressions are interpreted is not similar all over the world. [3] The interpretation of facial expressions changes from culture to culture. [4] People all over the world smile. [5] Everyone recognizes a smile as an expression of friendliness. [6] However, some cultures smile more often than others, and the cultures that smile less often might think that people who smile often are not sincere. [7] Some Northern European cultures feel this way about Americans who tend to smile too easily. [8] Another example of smiles being used in a culture-specific way is in Asia. [9] People smile there when they feel nervous or anxious. [10] Very few other cultures do this. [11] This type of smile is not understood well outside of Asia. [12] Eastern and Western people focus on different parts of the face to read each other's facial expressions. [13] For example, Chinese people tend to focus more on a person's eyes. [14] Westerners tend to focus more on a person's mouth and eyebrows. [15] Finally, different cultures have different social rules about eye contact. [16] In America, for example, it is critical to maintain eye contact. [17] In some countries, it is considered rude to make eye contact with a teacher or a boss.

1. Combine sentences 1 and 2 with the conjunction *but*. Delete the repeated phrase *similar all over the world* from the end of the new sentence.

2. Start sentence 3 with *In fact* to show that this sentence emphasizes the point in sentences 1 and 2.

3. Start sentence 4 with *For example*.

4. Combine sentences 4 and 5 with the conjunction *and* to connect the ideas.

5. Add a comma and *in their opinion* to the end of sentence 7 to emphasize that this is not the writer's opinion.

6. Start sentence 9 with *In some Asian countries* and delete *there* for clarity.

7. Combine sentences 10 and 11 with the conjunction *so* to emphasize the cause-effect relationship.

8. Begin sentence 12 with *Another difference is that.*

9. Combine sentences 13 and 14 with *but* to emphasize contrast.

10. Combine sentences 16 and 17 with *but* to emphasize contrast.

ACTIVITY 11   Original Writing

On a separate sheet of paper, write a comparison paragraph (at least six sentences) about two things that interest you. Explain what the two things are, and show how they are similar or different. Use facts, details, or examples. Use at least one example of a compound sentence with *but, and,* or *so* and underline it; try to use two if possible.

Here are some examples of how to begin.

- *The Philippine Eagle and the American Bald Eagle are very different in several ways.*

- *Reading novels and watching movies are both ways to relax, but most teenagers prefer watching movies.*

- *Cricket and American baseball are completely different games although they both involve hitting a ball with a bat.*

A worker in Ireland secures new straw thatching to a roof.

11 Using Parallel Structure

WHAT DO YOU KNOW?

DISCUSS Look at the photo and read the caption. Discuss the questions.

1. What do you think of this roof? Is it warm, attractive, or safe? Why, or why not?
2. What materials are traditionally used to build homes in your country?

FIND THE ERRORS This paragraph contains two errors with parallel structure. Find the errors and correct them. Explain your corrections to a partner.

DESCRIPTIVE PARAGRAPH

Thatched Roofs in England

[1] *Thatching* is a very old process for making roofs out of straw or grass. [2] Because thatch was light, cheap, and easily available, it was the most common roofing material in England until the end of the 19th century. [3] Starting in the late 1800s, most thatched roofs were replaced with slate, a material made from rock. [4] These days, however, thatched roofs are popular among people who want a traditional look or they are interested in using earth-friendly building materials. [5] Thatched roofs are valued both for their strength and beautiful. [6] A well-built roof can last up to 70 years. [7] On the other hand, a new thatched roof is expensive to install, and insurance is costly because thatched roofs have an increased risk of fire. [8] Despite these drawbacks, thatched roofs are a familiar sight in the English countryside. [9] One source estimates that there are more than 60,000 thatched roof buildings in Great Britain today.

Grammar Forms

11.1 Parallelism with Coordinating Conjunctions

Parallelism means that each item in a list has the same grammatical structure. Parallelism can occur in sets of words, phrases, and clauses. Use parallelism with items before and after coordinating conjunctions. Use it with:

1. words	The official languages of Switzerland are <u>German</u>, <u>French</u>, <u>Italian</u>, **and** <u>Romansh</u>. (*nouns*)
	Wild pearls, which grow naturally inside oysters, are <u>rare</u> **and** <u>expensive</u>. (*adjectives*)
	<u>Gardening</u>, <u>fishing</u>, **and** <u>bowling</u> are popular hobbies in the United States. (*gerunds*)
2. phrases	Most people brush their teeth twice a day, <u>in the morning</u> **and** <u>at night</u>. (*prepositional phrases*)
	Shakespeare's character Hamlet said, "<u>To be</u> **or** <u>not to be</u>, that is the question." (*infinitives*)
3. clauses	Scientists can predict <u>when a hurricane will arrive</u> **and** <u>how strong it will be</u>. (*noun clauses*)
	Reptiles are animals <u>that have cold blood</u> **and** <u>(that) live on land</u>. (*adjective clauses*)
	More and more young people are taking a year off <u>after they graduate from high school</u> **and** <u>before they start college</u>. (*adverb clauses*)

Note
When there are three or more parallel items, place a comma before *and*.
   To lose weight, one should avoid excess sugar, fat, and carbohydrates.

11.2 Parallelism with Correlative Conjunctions

Correlative conjunctions are used with two items that are equal in importance or weight. The structures before and after correlative conjunctions need to be parallel.

1. *both . . . and*	Shoes with very high heels are **both** <u>uncomfortable</u> **and** <u>unsafe</u>.
2. *either . . . or*	In national parks, the best time to photograph animals is **either** <u>in the early morning</u> **or** <u>in the late afternoon</u>.
3. *neither . . . nor*	The Jordan River is **neither** <u>deep</u> **nor** <u>wide</u>.

11.3 Parallelism in Comparisons

Use parallelism with items in comparisons. Use it with:

1. *as . . . as*	<u>Taking the train across the United States</u> can be **as** expensive **as** <u>flying</u>.
2. *more / less than*	<u>The cost of buying a new house</u> is often **more than** <u>the cost of remodeling an old one</u>. <u>The cost of remodeling an old house</u> is often **less than** <u>the cost of buying a new one</u>.

ACTIVITY 1

Underline the parallel elements in each sentence. Then label each conjunction with a *C*.

1. The traditional Mexican drink *horchata* contains rice, milk, water, vanilla, cinnamon, and sugar.

2. The character Superman has appeared in films, on television, and in comic books.

3. Many lines on the New York City subway system have both express and local trains.

4. In dry climates, gardens should be planted after the summer heat ends and before the fall rains begin.

5. At the age of five months, babies can neither walk nor talk.

6. An applicant for a passport needs to fill out an application, show proof of citizenship, show ID, submit a photo, and pay a fee.

7. No one can predict where a tornado will strike or how powerful it will be.

8. The liver is the organ that cleans the blood and that produces bile, which helps the body digest fat.

9. Throughout history, people have used horses for riding, for carrying heavy loads, and for pulling wagons and carriages.

10. Male singing voices are usually classified as either tenor (high) or bass (low).

Common Uses

11.4 Using Parallelism

Parallel structure in a sentence makes ideas balanced and clear. It is used in:

1. topic sentences and thesis statements • Thesis statements often include three parallel items that will be discussed.	Tablets are preferable to laptop computers because of their <u>cost</u>, <u>ease of use</u>, and <u>portability</u>.
2. lists of related items	Juneau, the capital of Alaska, can be reached <u>by sea</u> and <u>by air</u>, but not <u>by land</u>.
3. a series of actions	The three events in a typical triathlon are <u>swimming</u>, <u>cycling</u>, and <u>running</u>.
4. paired conjunctions (such as *both... and; either... or*) or comparisons (especially with *than* and *as . . . as*) • Comparisons must be between similar items.	The <u>scores of students in Group A</u> were greater **than** <u>the scores of students in Group B</u>. In São Paolo, Brazil, <u>November</u> is **as** hot **as** <u>December</u>. Juneau can be reached **either** <u>by sea</u> **or** <u>by air</u>.

ACTIVITY 2

Circle the letter of the choice that correctly forms a sentence with parallel structure.

1. Physiologists recommend a physical workout that combines stretching, _____, and cardio training.

    a. lift weights   **b.** lifting weights   **c.** to lift weights   *gerunds*

2. Some professors give students the choice to work _____, in pairs, or in groups.

    a. individual   **b.** by themselves   **c.** themselves   *prep + noun*

3. This study tracked the dental health of patients who brushed their teeth manually <u>compared to</u> _____ electric toothbrushes.

    a. patients who used   **b.** they used   **c.** using   *noun + adj clause*

4. Consumer Reports compared over 30 packaged cereals in terms of nutrition, package size, and _____.

    a. cost   **b.** how much it cost   **c.** what it cost   *nouns*

5. For many people, adding and subtracting mentally is faster than _____ a calculator.

    a. using   **b.** to use   **c.** use   *gerunds*

6. In general, high-tech jobs require more education than _____.

   a. manufacturing   **b.** manufacture the jobs   **c.** manufacturing jobs   *adj + noun*

7. Registered nurses must both _____ from nursing school and pass a difficult licensing exam.

   a. they graduate   **b.** graduation   **c.** graduate   *verb*

8. Tourists who want to visit China must do three things: fill out a visa application, get passport photos, and _____ an application packet to the Chinese embassy.

   a. submitting   **b.** submit   **c.** to submit   *verb*

ACTIVITY 3   *Hw on a paper.*

Complete the sentences with parallel items. Use the kind of item in parentheses and your own ideas.

1. Three popular activities among college students are _____, _____, and _____. (*gerunds*)

2. The ideal manager is _____, _____, and _____. (*adjectives*)

3. The ideal employee works _____ and _____. (*adverbs*)

4. _____, _____, and _____ are popular pets for people who live in apartments. (*nouns*)

5. To pass the time on long train or bus rides, passengers can _____, _____, or _____. (*verbs*)

6. These days, many people use cell phones _____, _____, and _____. (*infinitives*)

7. Many people enjoy drinking coffee either _____ or _____. (*prepositional phrases of time*)   *in the afternoon   at night on the week day*

8. An employee who commutes long distances needs a car _____ and _____. (*adjective clauses*)

Common Errors

Common Error 11.1   Are items parallel before and after a conjunction?

revising

Writing well requires planning, composing, and ~~you have to revise~~.

REMEMBER: Items before and after conjunctions should have the same grammatical structure.

ACTIVITY 4   **Common Error 11.1**

There is one parallelism error in each sentence. Underline and correct the error.

1. College students can live at home, in a campus dormitory, or ~~renting~~ an apartment. *prep + noun*

2. Two-thirds of the people surveyed said they thought married people were happier, healthier, and ~~they were~~ more fulfilled than unmarried people. *comparative adj*

3. The most common advice for treating a cold is to rest, drink hot liquids, and ~~taking~~ vitamin C. *(Inf)* *take*

4. Scientific experiments on animals can be justified if they will save human lives, end human suffering, and ~~there will be contributions~~ to science. *verb* *contribute*

5. A snake moves in a serpentine (S-shaped) movement by contracting its muscles, thrusting its body from side to side, and ~~it creates~~ a series of curves. *gerunds* *creating*

6. For years, mountain gorillas in Uganda have been threatened by habitat loss, disease, and ~~there is~~ illegal hunting. *noun*

7. High ticket prices, noisy patrons, and ~~the fact that there is~~ limited parking are three reasons why many people have stopped going to movie theaters. *noun*

8. Cinnamon is useful for flavoring food, lowering blood sugar, covering up bad smells, and ~~even eliminate~~ ants. *eliminating* *gerund*

Common Error 11.2   Are items after each part of a correlative conjunction parallel?

as a painter

Leonardo da Vinci was famous not only as an inventor but also ~~he was a painter~~.

REMEMBER: Items following each part of a conjunction should have the same grammatical structure.

Fill in the blank with the word or phrase that makes the sentence parallel.

1. Cloning human beings is both unethical and _____risky_____ (*it is risky / risky / a risk*).

2. In the Maldives and other low-lying islands threatened by rising sea levels, residents must either _____move_____ (*move / moving / to move*) to higher ground or emigrate to other countries.

3. Researchers say that spending too much time online both decreases a person's productivity and _____disrupts_____ (*it disrupts / disrupts / is disruptive*) family relationships.

4. Musicians flying with valuable instruments can either buy an extra ticket and carry the instrument on board or _____check_____ (*checking / check / they can check*) the instrument as baggage.

5. The word "glocal" is applied to business practices and products that are neither global nor _____local_____ (*local / they are local / are they local*). Rather, they are a combination of the two. For example, McDonald's includes some Japanese dishes on its menus in Japan.

6. Experts believe that global warming will bring more rain both to areas that are normally wet and _____ (*to areas that are normally dry / areas that are normally dry / areas they are normally dry*).

7. Chlorine bleach can be used to kill bacteria and ___to whiten clothes___ (*it whitens clothes / whitens clothes / to whiten clothes*).

8. High school students can earn college credits either by passing Advanced Placement tests or _____taking_____ (*they take / by taking / taking*) college courses along with their high school classes.

Common Error 11.3 Are items in a comparison parallel?

the population of Canada

According to recent statistics, the population of California is greater than ~~Canada~~.

REMEMBER: In a comparison, the items before and after *than* and *as* should have the same grammatical structure. Comparisons must be between similar items.

Each sentence has an error with parallel comparison. Underline the items that are compared. Edit the sentence to make the sentence parallel. For some sentences, more than one answer is possible.

1. Working in the garden can burn as many calories as a jog. *[jogging]*

2. Flying a short distance often takes more time than to drive. *[driving]*

3. In the past, it was unusual for a husband's income to be smaller than his wife. *[wife's income]*

4. The number of exams in undergraduate courses is usually greater than graduate courses. *[the number of exams in]*

5. Generally, a nurse's income is smaller than a doctor. *[doctor's income]*

6. The pronunciation of the letter *R* in Spanish is the same as Italian. *[in]*

7. Since 2013, the cost of housing in the United States has risen faster than food, transportation, or health care. *[the cost of]*

8. The cost of living in Tokyo is higher than Los Angeles. *[the cost of living in]*

A family relaxes together in their small Tokyo apartment.

Academic Vocabulary

Words from the Academic Word List (Sublist 6)

accurate	brief	exceed	gender	migration
author	enhanced	fees	intelligence	revealed

Source: Academic Word List (Coxhead 2000)

ACTIVITY 7 **Vocabulary in Academic Writing**

Use the academic vocabulary to complete the sentences. Notice the parallel structures.

Subject Area	Example from Academic Writing
Medicine	**1.** Scientists at Stanford University announced the development of a fast, inexpensive, and _____ way to test newborn babies for cystic fibrosis.
Astronomy	**2.** Johannes Kepler's scientific work ___brief_____ how humans see and what happens when light enters a telescope.
Education	**3.** This chapter will provide a ___revealed___ definition of three types of reading strategies.
Neuroscience	**4.** Dr. Robert Sternberg of Tufts University believes that people have three types of ___intelligence___: analytic, creative, and practical.
Psychology	**5.** A study of 866 Buddhists who practiced mindfulness meditation showed that the activity ___enhanced___ both physical and psychological health.
Geography	**6.** ___Migration___ from rural areas to cities occurs either because unfavorable local conditions push people to leave or because attractive opportunities in cities pull people to come.
English Composition	**7.** Drivers may ___exceed___ the speed limit because they are in a hurry, they enjoy speed, or they are bored.
English Literature	**8.** Maya Angelou was an award-winning American ___author___, poet, and civil rights activist.
Sociology	**9.** In a 2014 survey by the Pew Research Center, 74 percent of men and 76 percent of women said that a person of either ___gender___ could be an effective political leader.
Education	**10.** At most universities, ___fees___ cover the cost of registration and tuition, but they do not cover books or housing.

Put It Together

Review Quiz

Multiple Choice Choose the letter of the correct answer.

1. Many television viewers enjoy programs that are both entertaining and _____.

   a. educate   **b.** they educate   **c.** educational   **d.** education

2. Artificial sweeteners like sucralose neither raise blood sugar levels nor _____ tooth decay.

   a. cause   **b.** they cause   **c.** do cause   **d.** causing

3. Golf requires flexibility, coordination, and _____.

   a. concentrate   **b.** concentration   **c.** to concentrate   **d.** concentrating

4. A house in Philadelphia is cheaper than _____.

   a. Manhattan   **b.** is in Manhattan   **c.** a house in Manhattan   **d.** Manhattan's houses

5. For a long time, educators have been asking if grades discourage students or _____ them to work harder.

   a. do they motivate   **b.** they motivate   **c.** motivating   **d.** motivate

Error Correction One of the five underlined words or phrases is not correct. Find the error and correct it. Be prepared to explain your answer.

6. People can conserve water indoors by taking shorter showers, turn off the faucet while brushing their teeth, and fixing leaks in the plumbing. To save water outdoors, people with gardens are encouraged to replace grass lawns with low-water plants and avoid over-watering.

7. Eating more fruits and vegetables, exercising regularly, and maintaining close personal relationships are three steps that can lower the risk of developing cancer, heart disease, or becoming depressed.

8. Children who are exposed to reading at a young age develop essential skills that help prepare them for school and for learning. Among other abilities, they learn how to recognize cause and effect, identifying feelings, and make judgments based on the behavior of characters in stories.

ACTIVITY 9   **Building Greater Sentences**

Combine these short sentences into one sentence. You can add new words and move words around, but you should not add or omit any ideas. More than one answer is possible, but these sentences require parallelism.

1. a. A zebra's stripes help it to keep cool.
   b. A zebra's stripes help it avoid insect bites.
   c. A zebra's stripes help it hide from predators such as lions.

_____

_____

2. a. In 2024, the Summer Olympics will happen.
   b. Maybe the Summer Olympics will be in Europe.
   c. Maybe the Summer Olympics will be in North America

_____

_____

3. a. Alexander Hamilton was the first United States Secretary of the Treasury.
   b. He was the founder of the Federalist Party.
   c. The Federalist Party was the first democratic political party in the world.

_____

_____

Steps to Composing

Read the paragraph. Then follow the directions in the 10 steps to edit the information and composition of this paragraph. Write your revised paragraph on a separate sheet of paper. Be careful with capitalization and punctuation. Check your answers with the class.

CLASSIFICATION PARAGRAPH

Levels of Airline Service

[1] For long-distance flights, all airlines these days offer three levels of service. [2] They are Economy Class, Business Class, and First Class. [3] These levels differ in price and comfort. [4] As most tourists know, Economy Class is the cheapest but also the least comfortable level of service. [5] It is also known as Coach. [6] Seats are narrow and legroom is tight. [7] On many airlines, passengers must pay extra to reserve a specific seat or check an extra bag. [8] One solution is to pay five times more and fly Business Class. [9] In Business Class, the seats are wider. [10] In Business Class, there is more legroom. [11] The food and service are superior. [12] If these luxuries are not enough, travelers can choose to fly First Class. [13] They can enjoy private suites, gourmet food, showers, and even massages. [14] However, this level of service is expensive. [15] A ticket in First Class can cost twice as much as Business Class and up to twenty times as much as Economy Class.

1. In sentence 1, add the word *nearly* before *all airlines* for accuracy.

2. Sentence 2 lists the three levels of service in sentence 1. Combine the sentences by replacing the period in sentence 1 with a colon. Delete *They are* from sentence 2.

3. In sentence 3, add the word *both* after *differ* for emphasis.

4. In sentence 4, add the adjective clause *which is also known as Coach Class* after *Economy Class*. Place commas before and after the adjective clause. Delete sentence 5.

5. The word *level* is used in sentences 3 and 4. For variety, change it to *class* in sentence 4.

6. Combine sentences 9 and 10 into one sentence. Delete *In Business Class* from sentence 10, and add the conjunction *and*.

7. In sentence 12, add the word *wealthy* before *travelers*.

8. Combine sentences 12 and 13 by adding the word *where*.

9. Move *However* to the end of sentence 14.

10. In sentence 15, add *a ticket in* before *Business Class* and before *Economy Class* for parallelism.

Original Writing

On a separate sheet of paper, write a classification paragraph (at least six sentences). Classify one topic into three categories and give facts, details, and/or examples. Use at least two examples of parallelism.

Here are some examples of how to begin:

- *A balanced workout includes aerobic exercise, strength training, and stretching.*
- *The most common causes of stress for students are poor sleep habits, academic pressure, and weak time management skills.*
- *College students can choose to live in a dormitory, in an apartment off-campus, or with family.*

Siblings at home in Glendale, California, play with their tablet computers.

12 Using Passive Voice

WHAT DO YOU KNOW?

DISCUSS   Look at the photo and read the caption. Discuss the questions.

1. What did you play with when you were a child? What do children play with today?

2. What do you think might cause headaches in children?

FIND THE ERRORS   This paragraph contains two errors with the passive voice. Find the errors and correct them. Explain your corrections to a partner.

CAUSE-EFFECT PARAGRAPH

Headaches in Children

^{1}A surprising number of children as young as four or five suffer from headaches regularly. ^{2}There are a variety of factors that could be causing these headaches from stress to too much screen time. ^{3}To have a better idea of the causes of a child's headaches, parents could try to keep a journal of when headaches occur. ^{4}However, before getting too concerned, pediatricians suggest that parents try to make some simple changes. ^{5}For example, some children's headaches are caused by not getting enough sleep at night. ^{6}Children who are still taken naps during the day may sleep better without them. ^{7}Headaches can also occur when young children are not fed at regular intervals or are not gave enough water to drink. ^{8}Pediatricians usually suggest that parents try these changes before giving their children headache medication.

Grammar Forms

12.1 Passive Voice

In a passive sentence, the receiver of the action is in the subject position.

Active voice: The doctor **examined** the child.
                              S   V   O

Passive voice: The child **was examined** (by the doctor).
                              S   V

Verb Form	*Be* + Past Participle	Example
1. Simple present	*am / is / are* + (*not*) + past participle	New cars **are tested** before they **are delivered** to the market. New cars **are not delivered** to the market before they **are tested**.
2. Simple past	*was / were* + (*not*) + past participle	A new species of wild tomato **was discovered** recently. Tomatoes **were not grown** in England until the late 16th century.
3. Present perfect	*has / have* + (*not*) + *been* + past participle	Drones, or unmanned aerial vehicles, **have been used** by the American military since World War I. An accurate way to predict earthquakes **has not been found.**
4. Modals	modal + (*not*) + *be* + past participle	Many coastal cities **may be affected** by rising seas in the future. Pets **should not be left** in cars in hot weather.

Notes

1. Only transitive verbs (verbs that can have a direct object) can be made passive.

2. The form of *be* or *have/has* agrees with the subject of the sentence.

3. For passive modals, the base form of *be* is used and the modal form does not change.

4. Progressive passives are rarely used in academic writing.

5. See Appendix 4, Irregular Verbs, page 220, for irregular past participles.

Fill in the blanks with the passive forms of the words in parentheses.

1. Although Amelia Earhart's plane crash happened in 1937, the exact reasons for the plane

crash _____ (present perfect: *not / uncover*).

2. In the past, people often said that children _____

(simple present: *should / see*) and not heard, but that is not how most people raise their

children today.

3. More children in the USA _____ (present perfect: *diagnose*)

with diabetes in this decade than in previous decades.

4. Thirteen hundred pounds of Roman coins in very good condition from the third or fourth

centuries _____ (simple past: *find*) by Spanish workers in

2016 while they were digging up water lines.

5. In some private and public schools, children with mild or moderate learning disabilities

_____ (simple present: *give*) tutors who stay with them for

most of the day.

6. Many places _____ (simple past: *not / discover*) deliberately

but rather _____ (simple past: *find*) by accident when early

explorers' ships _____ (simple past: *blow*) off course by

strong winds.

7. A common cause of stress in many workplaces today is when too many things

_____ (simple present: *have to / complete*) at the same

time and there is not enough time to complete them.

8. The International Space Station _____ (simple present:

can / observe) crossing the night skies several times a year.

Common Uses

12.2 Using Passive Voice

The passive voice is commonly used in writing when the doer of the action (or agent) is not known or not important. It is used:

1. to focus attention on the action of the sentence	YouTube **was founded** in 2005.
2. to focus attention on the receiver(s) of the action	The participants **were given** questionnaires as they entered the room.
3. to give the sequence of events	In 1996, the first cell phone with Internet access **was made** available to the public.
4. to explain a process	First, all the materials **are taken out of** the refrigerator and allowed to warm up. Then the liquid nitrogen **is poured** into a test tube.
5. to avoid direct criticism or blame	Mistakes **were made** in the research project proposal.
6. to make a statement less personal with *it is known / thought / considered*	It **is considered** rude to stare at a person.

Notes

1. Use *by* + the agent only when it is important to know who the agent is.

   Fireworks **were invented** in ancient China. (There is no need to include *by inventors*.)

   Fireworks **should not be handled** by children.

2. Only transitive verbs (verbs that take a direct object) can be made passive. Intransitive verbs (verbs that do not take direct objects, such as *work*, *exist*, or *happen*) cannot be made passive.

   A full moon always **rises** just as the sun **is setting**. (The verbs are intransitive, so no passive form is possible.)

Underline the passive verb forms. In some sentences, there is more than one passive construction.

1. The International Space Station <u>was first launched</u> in 1998.

2. American women <u>were not given</u> the right to vote until 1920.

3. The new president <u>has been advised</u> not to meet with the protestors, but that may have been a mistake.

4. It can take a long time to create a new law. First, an idea, or a bill, <u>is introduced</u> by a member of congress. Then <u>it is debated</u> by various committees.

5. No one knows exactly when shoelaces <u>were first invented</u>, but <u>it is thought</u> that they were in use as far back as 3500 BCE.

6. Many mistakes <u>were made</u> in the early days of the development of the Apple computer.

7. When parents get divorced, often children are too young <u>to be told</u> the real reasons for the divorce.

8. To learn about the density of ice, ice cubes <u>are dropped</u> into a glass of cooking oil so that students can observe what happens to the ice as it melts.

ACTIVITY 3

Label the underlined verbs in these active sentences *T* (transitive) or *I* (intransitive). Then rewrite the sentences with transitive verbs as passive sentences. Add *by* phrases only when necessary.

1. The Norwegian Nobel Committee <u>awarded</u> the Nobel Peace Prize to Juan Manuel Santos of Colombia in 2016.

_____

2. Native Americans <u>burned</u> areas of open land to protect crops from wild animals.

_____

3. In the United States, many children <u>enjoy</u> organized sports programs.

_____

4. Droughts in the Southwestern United States <u>are occurring</u> more frequently.

_____

5. Some online news outlets <u>reported</u> the results of the elections inaccurately at first.

_____

6. People in 25 different countries <u>speak</u> Arabic as a primary language.

_____

Common Errors

Common Error 12.1 Is the passive missing a form of *be*?

are
Camels ‸used for transportation in the desert because they can survive without drinking water for a very long time.

REMEMBER: All passive sentences have a form of *be* + past participle.

ACTIVITY 4 Common Error 12.1

There is one incorrect passive form in each sentence. Underline and correct the incorrect passive form.

1. In 2015, more than 15,000 drones sold every month in the United States.

2. Many people think that consultants paid more than employees, but this is not always true.

3. More children left alone at home after school in the last decade because their parents have been busy working.

4. Neuroscientists think that some Alzheimer's patients' memories can retrieved with a specific type of brain stimulation.

5. Many mountainous areas have search and rescue teams that used to help hikers who get lost or hurt.

6. Engineers paid higher salaries than education professionals such as teachers or school counselors.

7. Children who praised at school often perform better than children who criticized.

8. For years, thousands of young people have arrived in Los Angeles every year with hopes to become actors, but very few given the opportunities they need to succeed

9. Artificial food coloring added to farmed salmon to make it look like freshwater salmon.

10. House plants often die either because they not watered enough or they are overwatered.

Common Error 12.2 Is the passive form correct?

were robbed   *were broken*
After Hurricane Katrina, many stores ~~was rob~~ and houses ~~was broke~~ into.

REMEMBER: Use the form of *be* or *have/has* that agrees with the subject of the sentence, and use the past participle form of the verb.

ACTIVITY 5 **Common Error 12.2**

Fill in the blanks with the correct passive forms of the verbs in parentheses.

1. Some genetic diseases _____ (simple present: *carry*) from one generation to the next, while others skip a generation.

2. In solar cells, sunlight _____ (simple present: *transform*) into electricity.

3. The migration of the monarch butterfly is so difficult and dangerous that many butterflies _____ (modal: *can / lose*) during each stage.

4. Parts of the Great Wall of China _____ (present progressive: *destroy*) gradually by sandstorms, and _____ (modal: *may / go*) in under 20 years.

5. Studies show that original ideas _____ (simple present: *form*) in more than one part of the brain at the same time.

6. Hippocrates _____ (simple present: *know*) as the father of modern medicine because he was the first doctor to use science instead of magic to heal people.

7. Velcro _____ (simple past: *not / invent*) deliberately but rather by accident when a Swiss scientist noticed the structure of the burrs sticking to his clothes.

8. Some psychologists think that the millennial generation _____ (present perfect: *give*) too much praise over the years.

Common Error 12.3   Do you need passive or active voice?

      were
The students ˄recognized for their excellent work.

      worked
They ~~are worked~~ at the laboratory until late at night.

REMEMBER: • Use the active voice if the subject of the sentence is doing the action. Use the passive voice if the subject is receiving the action.

      • Intransitive verbs do not have objects. Therefore, they cannot be used in the passive voice.

Underline the verb forms that correctly complete the paragraphs.

1.   One of the first places modern yoga (*saw / was seen*) in the West was at the World's Fair in the 1890s. It (*was performed / performed*) by an Indian named Swami Vivekananda. The Swami also (*gave / was given*) a speech. In his speech, he (*was talked / talked*) about world religions and a universal religion. Swami Vivekananda's presence at the World's Fair (*was / was been*) the beginning of the popularity of yoga in the United States.

2.   Bacteria and other organisms (*can be found / can find*) living on every surface of the world. One way biologists (*are studied / study*) bacteria is by using controlled conditions. They take a sample and (*are grown / grow*) it in the laboratory. However, some types of bacteria are actually invisible, so they (*cannot be grown / cannot grow*) by biologists in controlled conditions. For this reason, it has been very difficult for biologists to study these types of bacteria. However, recently a new method of DNA sequencing (*has been successfully used / has successfully used*) to study this invisible bacteria. Scientists (*hope / are hoped*) that this new method of studying invisible bacteria will continue to reveal very useful information.

3.   The Pacific Garbage Patch is a mass of plastic garbage that (*has collected / has been collected*) together in the middle of the Pacific Ocean as an island of garbage. It is a very very big island. In fact, it (*is estimated / estimated*) to be the same size as the United States. How was this "garbage island" (*form / formed*)? First, garbage (*threw / was thrown*) into streams, rivers, and oceans. Then the garbage (*picked up / was picked up*) by ocean currents and brought to this area. Many people (*have tried / have been tried*) to figure out how to fix this problem, but so far there are no good solutions.

4.   A new study (*shows / is shown*) that participating in sports activities while studying at a college or university (*can improve / can be improved*) your grades. This study (*done / was done*) in Spain. The grades of 3,671 students (*were collected / collected*) over a period of approximately seven years. The students who (*were participated / participated*) in sports achieved GPAs that were an average of nine points higher than the students who (*were not participated / did not participate*) in sports.

Academic Vocabulary

Passive Verb Forms Frequently Used in Academic Writing

are based	can be used	is needed	was reported	were conducted
can be seen	is known	was made	were asked	were found

Source: Corpus of Contemporary American English (Davies 2008–)

ACTIVITY 7   **Vocabulary in Academic Writing**

Use the academic vocabulary in the passive forms given to complete the sentences. For some sentences, more than one answer is possible.

Subject Area	Example from Academic Writing
Food Sciences	**1.** Even though it _____ that artificial sweeteners may cause cancer, they are still widely used.
Health Sciences	**2.** According to recent studies, it is possible that coconut oil with added enzymes _____ to prevent tooth decay.
Geology	**3.** There are many theories explaining why the dinosaurs became extinct, but more information _____ about the rocks deep below the earth's surface before scientists know for sure.
Biology	**4.** New studies _____ to determine if sweat samples can give doctors the same reliable information about people's health as their blood samples.
Psychology	**5.** When parents _____ about their children's sleep patterns, the information that they gave was usually different from the information the scientists got.
Archeology	**6.** Small pieces of wood attached to Neanderthal teeth _____ by archeologists recently, leading them to conclude that Neanderthals might have used toothpicks.
Government	**7.** After much discussion, a decision _____ to focus on youth and unemployment for the next five years.
Medicine	**8.** Many good doctors will tell you that their decisions _____ not only on science, but on intuition, as well.
Sociology	**9.** The data on the average age of marriage among people born after 1985 _____ in table 4.
Political Science	**10.** The election between the two candidates _____ as a tie on television, but that information was not correct.

Put It Together

ACTIVITY 8   **Review Quiz**

Multiple Choice   Choose the letter of the correct answer.

1. In 1929, a global depression _____ by the U.S. stock market crash.

   a. were caused   **b.** caused   **c.** was caused   **d.** was causing

2. Most parents have to ask their children repeatedly to help around the house, while some children are happy to help their parents as soon as they _____.

   a. are asked   **b.** been asked not   **c.** be asked   **d.** were not asked

3. Many of Michelangelo's paintings _____ inspired by Greek and Roman myths.

   a. are being   **b.** were   **c.** may be   **d.** was

4. Traveling to other countries often _____ people's lives.

   a. changes   **b.** was changed   **c.** were changed   **d.** was changing

5. Antibiotics _____ overused over the past few decades and as a result have caused the development of antibiotic-resistant bacteria.

   a. was   **b.** cannot be   **c.** may not be   **d.** have been

Error Correction One of the five underlined words or phrases is not correct. Find the error and correct it. Be prepared to explain your answer.

6. Many people <u>think</u> the desert <u>is</u> always brown, but the flowers that <u>are seen</u> in the

   desert after <u>even</u> just a very short rain shower often <u>are changed</u> the landscape into

   a beautiful rainbow of colors.

7. <u>For</u> those who want to try home remedies, herbalists suggest that peppermint oil

   <u>be use</u> instead <u>of</u> over-the-counter medications <u>to soothe</u> a sore throat.

8. <u>All dogs</u> enjoy <u>going</u> for walks <u>in parks</u> and <u>on beaches</u>, especially where leashes

   <u>are not require</u>.

ACTIVITY 9　Building Greater Sentences

Combine these short sentences into one sentence. You can add new words and move words around, but you should not add or omit any ideas. More than one answer is possible, but all of these sentences require both the passive and the active voice.

1. a. Human sleep patterns are regulated by exposure to light.
   b. Light is recognized by a part of the brain.
   c. This part of the brain tells people that it is time to be awake.

_____

_____

2. a. There is a new material for making clothes.
   b. This material is environmentally friendly.
   c. This new material is made from mushrooms.
   d. The clothes can be recycled and reused.

_____

_____

3. a. A healthy environment is necessary.
   b. The environment should be protected.
   c. Every country in the world should protect it.

_____

_____

Steps to Composing

Read the classification paragraph. Then follow the directions in the 10 steps to edit the information and composition of this paragraph. Write your revised paragraph on a separate sheet of paper. Be careful with capitalization and punctuation. Check your answers with the class.

CLASSIFICATION PARAGRAPH

Elements of an Effective Apology

[1] Apologizing can be a difficult thing to do. [2] According to recent research, an effective apology needs to contain various elements. [3] However, there are two elements that people consider more important than all the others. [4] For an apology to be effective, it should include an admission of responsibility. [5] Some people apologize with an excuse for their action, saying for example, "I'm sorry, but I was tired," or "I'm sorry, but I didn't realize you would be bothered by . . ." [6] In these apologies, there is no blame or responsibility. [7] What is heard is only an excuse. [8] This type of apology can make the offended person even more upset or angry. [9] Another element that should be included in an effective apology is an offer to fix the situation. [10] Offering to fix the situation shows that the apologizer has thought a lot about the offensive behavior. [11] It also shows that the apologizer has thought a lot about the offended person, too. [12] One common element of an apology that is not very helpful is to ask for forgiveness, so that part can be omitted.

---

1. Add *effectively* to the end of sentence 1 to better define the paragraph topic.

2. Combine sentences 2 and 3. Change the period between *element* and *However* to a semi-colon.

3. In sentence 3, *people* (the agent) is not that important. Change *people consider* to *are considered*.

4. Start sentence 4 with *First* and a comma to emphasize that this is the first element.

5. In sentence 6, change *there is no blame or responsibility* to the passive form *no blame or responsibility is communicated*.

6. In sentence 7, add *or justification* after *excuse*.

7. Start sentence 9 with *Second* and a comma to emphasize that this is the second element.

8. In sentence 10, change the subject to *this* to avoid repetition.

9. Sentences 10 and 11 have related ideas. Combine the sentences with *and*. Then delete *It also shows that the speaker has thought a lot about* and *too* to avoid repetition.

10. Add *both* to the new combined sentence for emphasis.

ACTIVITY 11   **Original Writing**

On a separate sheet of paper, write a classification paragraph (at least six sentences) about a topic that interests you. Explain what it is and give facts, details, and/or examples. Use at least one example of the passive voice and underline it; try to use two if possible.

Here are some examples of how to begin.

- *Most people have several different kinds of friends.*
- *An interesting presentation needs to include certain elements.*
- *Most people spend their vacation in one of three ways.*

A sixteen-year-old giant panda rests at the Wolong National Nature Reserve, Sichuan Province, China.

13 Using Gerunds and Infinitives

WHAT DO YOU KNOW?

DISCUSS Look at the photo and read the caption. Discuss the questions.

1. Have you ever seen a panda or other endangered animal? Why are these animals endangered?

2. How can people help protect endangered animals?

FIND THE ERRORS This paragraph contains two errors with gerunds or infinitives. Find the errors and correct them. Explain your corrections to a partner.

PROCESS PARAGRAPH

Saving Wildlife

[1] In the process of trying to save endangered species, many wildlife organizations turn to governments, businesses, and local communities for help. [2] The first, and perhaps most important, step in saving plants and animals is to have as wide-reaching an impact as possible. [3] Because governments—national, regional, and local—can help the effort by passing laws for protect the wildlife and their habitats, organizations turn to them first. [4] Another step organizations can make is to contact businesses, both large and small. [5] For example, businesses can help endangered species by landscaping with native plants in their business parks. [6] Finally, a third step organizations can take is to work within their local communities. [7] By sponsoring fairs and educational events, local communities help increase awareness of the need to protect native species. [8] It is important to educate people about the wildlife in their community and to offer ways to protect the animals' habitat. [9] Work together is key if these animals are going to survive.

Grammar Forms

13.1 Gerunds

A gerund is the base form of the verb + -ing. It acts as a noun and can be in the subject or object position in a sentence.

Position	Example
1. as the subject of a sentence	**Exercising** just 30 minutes a day can lead to good heart health.
2. as the object of certain verbs	Many students avoid **making** outlines before they begin to write.
3. as the object of a preposition	Education majors look forward to **helping** students succeed.

13.2 Infinitives

An infinitive is *to* + base form of the verb. It is used:

Position	Example
1. after certain verbs	The company's marketing strategy failed **to attract** new customers.
2. in the construction *it* + *be* + adjective	It is possible **to receive** on-the-job training for some careers.

13.3 Negative Gerunds and Infinitives

The word *not* goes before a gerund or infinitive to make it negative.

Form	Example
not + gerund	**Not taking** time to relax increases one's stress level. Many students worry about **not finding** a job after they graduate.
not + infinitive	In order to address global warming, it is important **not to waste** water, food, or energy.

13.4 Gerunds or Infinitives after Verbs

Some verbs are followed by infinitives, some are followed by gerunds, and some are followed by gerunds or infinitives with no difference in meaning.

	Verb	Example
1. verb + gerund	avoid, consider, enjoy, finish, postpone, practice, quit, recommend, stop	Many students **avoid taking** English classes their first semester in college.
2. verb + infinitive	agree, ask, decide, hope, need, plan, refuse, seem, want	Because citizen input is important, many city councils **agree to give** citizens time to speak at council meetings.
3. verb + gerund or infinitive	begin, continue, hate, like, love, prefer, start	Today, many students **prefer taking** classes online. Today, many students **prefer to take** classes online.

ACTIVITY 1

Read the following sentences. If the underlined form is correct, write *C* on the line. If the underlined form is incorrect, write *X* on the line. Then write the correct form above the sentence. More than one correction may be possible.

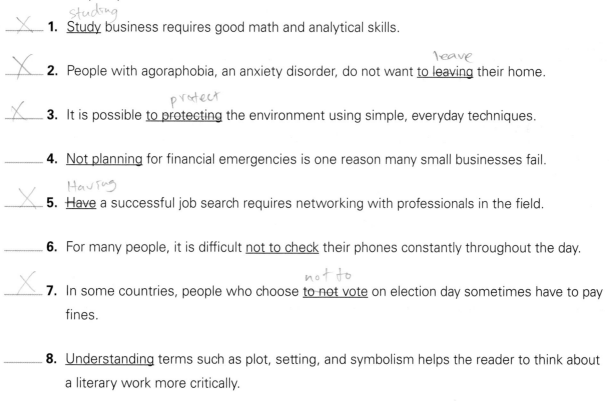

studying

__X__ **1.** <u>Study</u> business requires good math and analytical skills.

leave

__X__ **2.** People with agoraphobia, an anxiety disorder, do not want <u>to leaving</u> their home.

protect

__X__ **3.** It is possible <u>to protecting</u> the environment using simple, everyday techniques.

_____ **4.** <u>Not planning</u> for financial emergencies is one reason many small businesses fail.

Having

__X__ **5.** <u>Have</u> a successful job search requires networking with professionals in the field.

_____ **6.** For many people, it is difficult <u>not to check</u> their phones constantly throughout the day.

not to

__X__ **7.** In some countries, people who choose <u>to not vote</u> on election day sometimes have to pay fines.

_____ **8.** <u>Understanding</u> terms such as plot, setting, and symbolism helps the reader to think about a literary work more critically.

Common Uses

13.5 Using Gerunds

Gerunds (and gerund phrases) are commonly used in academic writing. They are used:

1. as the subject of a sentence	**Volunteering** is one of several ways to acquire job experience.
2. as the object of a preposition	The study focused on **finding** new methods to detect cancer. Researchers are interested in **conducting** further studies.
3. as the object of certain verbs	People dislike **speaking** in public for several reasons.
4. as a noun after the verb *be*	Students stated their favorite weekend activity was **sleeping late**.
5. after *by* (to explain how something is done)	Participants were divided into two groups by **selecting** names at random from a longer, larger list.

Notes
1. Gerund subjects are always singular.
2. Common verb + preposition + gerund combinations include *ask about, worry about, think of, count on, keep on,* and *succeed in.*
3. Common adjective + preposition + gerund combinations include *afraid of, good at, interested in, worried about,* and *responsible for.*

13.6 Using Infinitives

Infinitives (and infinitive phrases) are commonly used in academic writing. They are used:

1. as the object of the verb	The researchers intended **to show** which study habits were most successful.
2. after a form of the verb *be*	According to the survey, the main goal of most students is **to graduate** without a lot of debt.
3. after *it* + *be* + adjective	It is almost impossible **to predict** the outcome of some criminal trials.

Notes
1. Infinitives are not commonly used as subjects. Gerunds are more common.
2. Infinitives (*to* + verb) can be used to express purpose. They have the same meaning as *in order to* + verb.
   [In order] **To graduate** from college with no debt, many students work part time or even full time.
3. Common adjectives after *it* + *be* include *difficult, easy, important, impossible, interesting,* and *necessary.*

Fill in the blank with the correct gerund or infinitive form of the verb in parentheses. More than one answer may be possible.

1. _____Burning_____ (*burn*) fossil fuels, which releases carbon dioxide into the atmosphere, has harmful effects on the environment.

2. One reason many immigrants decide _____to become_____ (*become*) citizens is to have the right to vote.

3. It is not always easy _____to determine_____ (*determine*) whether information on the Internet is accurate.

4. Researchers were interested in _____learning_____ (*learn*) about the positive and negative effects of a high-protein diet on the body.

5. The first step in writing an essay is _____brainstorming_____ (*brainstorm*) ideas about the topic.

6. There are a number of reasons that people avoid _____to going_____ (*go*) to the dentist.

7. One needs time, money, and passion _____to succeed_____ (*succeed*) in business.

8. Studies indicate that by _____reviewing_____ (*review*) the questions in an exam before answering them, students achieve higher scores.

9. It is important _____to choose_____ (*choose*) a career for the satisfaction it brings rather than for the paycheck it brings.

10. _____Saving_____ (*save*) endangered animals is the mission of many environmental groups worldwide.

Common Errors

Common Error 13.1   Is the verb followed by an infinitive or a gerund?

>   *to find*
> Scientists hope ~~finding~~ a new medicine to fight this disease.
>
>   *staying*
> One good piece of advice for college students is to avoid ~~to stay~~ up all night to study.

REMEMBER: Certain verbs are followed by infinitives, and certain verbs are followed by gerunds.

ACTIVITY 3   Common Error 13.1

Underline the correct verb forms.

1. Many students plan (*paying / to pay*) for their college education in one of three ways: working part time, applying for financial aid, or getting loans.

2. Employers want (*increasing / to increase*) productivity and (*reducing / to reduce*) employee theft.

3. Therapists suggested (*finding / to find*) ways to meet one's own needs as well as others' needs.

4. There are several actions one can take to avoid (*to catch / catching*) a cold.

5. Forest service personnel want (*improving / to improve*) the ecosystem by overseeing controlled burns of forests.

6. A bachelor's degree in economics requires (*taking / to take*) courses in calculus and statistics.

7. Employers who refuse (*to give / giving*) their workers overtime pay may face lawsuits and fines.

8. Experts recommend (*to anticipate / anticipating*) possible test questions as a study skills strategy.

Common Error 13.2   Is the correct form used after a preposition?

>   *becoming*
> Many newly arrived immigrants dream about ~~to become~~ rich.
>
>   *hiring*
> As late as the mid-1940s, many business owners were opposed to ~~hire~~ women.
>
>   *setting*
> Small business owners can expand their businesses by ~~set~~ specific goals.

REMEMBER: • Use a gerund after a preposition.
                   • Use a gerund after a multi-word preposition (for example, *opposed to*).
                   • Use a gerund after *by* to show manner (for example, *by setting specific goals*).

Common Error 13.2

Read the following sentences. Each sentence contains an error. Underline and correct the error by replacing it with a gerund.

1. There are a number of reasons that people who are used to work alone have a difficult time working on a team.

2. Students limit their chances of obtaining gainful employment by drop out of college before getting a degree.

3. Whereas in the past, many people looked forward to retire at age 65, many people today continue working past the age of 70.

4. People interested in learn about the health care profession should consider volunteering at a hospital or clinic.

5. Fear of failure is one reason people put off to do things that need to be done.

6. Due to health concerns, consumer advocates insist on to know which foods are genetically modified organisms (GMOs).

7. One can become an active listener by master four simple steps.

8. Local law enforcement is responsible for enforce local laws, investigating crimes, and protecting the local population.

Common Error 13.3   Is the subject a gerund?

Obtaining
~~Obtain~~ oxygen from the environment is one important role of the respiratory system.

REMEMBER: Use a gerund, not the base form of the verb, as the subject.

ACTIVITY 5   **Common Error 13.3**

Underline the subject in each sentence. If the form is correct, write *C* on the line. If the form is incorrect, write *X* on the line. Then write the correct form above the subject.

_____ 1. Learn about a foreign country's customs can help visitors avoid behaving impolitely when traveling.

_____ 2. When businesses hire new workers, explaining the company's culture is one of several important steps to include during training.

_____ 3. Developing vaccines faster than the rate at which viruses change is the focus of numerous research grants today.

_____ **4.** Use technology to improve student comprehension of complex subjects is one of many methods instructors employ in the classroom.

_____ **5.** Because it requires no special equipment, walk is one of the easiest ways to lose weight.

_____ **6.** Checking the locks on doors more than once before going to bed is a common behavior, but it can interfere with daily life for people with obsessive-compulsive disorder.

Common Error 13.4   Is there a subject?

It is
~~Is~~ necessary to become a citizen in order to vote in an election.

REMEMBER: Use *it* as the subject in a sentence with an infinitive phrase.

Common Error 13.5   Is there a singular verb after a gerund or infinitive subject?

is
Participating in team sports ~~are~~ an example of a good way to make friends.

REMEMBER: Use a singular verb after a gerund or infinitive subject. Gerunds are much more common as subjects than infinitives.

ACTIVITY 6   Common Errors 13.4 and 13.5

Read the following sentences. If the sentence is correct, write *C* on the line. If the sentence is incorrect, write *X* on the line. Then correct the sentence.

_____ **1.** For many immigrants, is a difficult decision to leave their home country.

_____ **2.** It is interesting to travel to another country to experience the culture.

_____ **3.** Taking vitamins are an important part of many people's daily routine.

_____ **4.** Despite what some employees may think, is wrong to take work supplies home for personal use.

_____ **5.** It takes time and effort to change one's lifestyle, but it is not impossible to change.

_____ **6.** According to a recent survey, it is less expensive to eat healthful foods than to eat junk food.

_____ **7.** For residents who live along the coast, is important to be aware of rising sea levels.

_____ **8.** Finding cures for different types of cancer is the goal of medical researchers.

Academic Vocabulary

Verbs Frequently Used after Gerunds and Infinitives in Academic Writing

be	find	know	make	use
develop	have	learn	participate	work

Source: Corpus of Contemporary American English (Davies 2008–)

ACTIVITY 7 **Vocabulary in Academic Writing**

Use the academic vocabulary in the gerund or infinitive form to complete the sentences. For some sentences, more than one answer is possible.

Subject Area	Example from Academic Writing
History	1. Since 1960 and the Kennedy–Nixon debates, candidates for public office have usually agreed _____ in televised debates.
Health	2. It is often recommended that people with sleep disorders avoid _____ food or drink with caffeine shortly before bedtime in order to sleep better.
Political Science	3. There are several reasons some lawmakers want to consider _____ it illegal to use drones to monitor people without their consent.
Anthropology	4. Through their research, medical anthropologists expect _____ different cultural beliefs and practices related to medicine.
Business	5. People who do not enjoy _____ in a team environment might consider becoming technical writers, translators, or computer programmers.
Mathematics	6. Researchers are interested in _____ the challenges students face when learning advanced level mathematics.
Technology	7. The automotive industry, both domestic and foreign, is involved in _____ self-driving cars.
Education	8. Along with knowledge of the subject matter they teach, prospective educators need _____ creative, empathetic, and flexible.
Psychology	9. Psychologists commonly suggest _____ meditation as a way to reduce stress and anxiety.
Biology	10. Microbiologists study viruses, parasites, and bacteria because they want _____ how to find treatments for the diseases they cause.

Put It Together

Review Quiz

Multiple Choice   Choose the letter of the correct answer.

1. Advertising on social media has the advantage of _____ millions of potential customers.

   a. to reach   **b.** reach   **c.** to reaching   **d.** reaching

2. During good economic times, when employment rates are high, many people consider _____ their jobs and opening their own businesses.

   a. quit   **b.** to quit   **c.** quitting   **d.** to quitting

3. In a recent travel survey, 45 percent of the respondents said they planned _____ a week-long cruise during their next scheduled vacation.

   a. to take   **b.** taking   **c.** take   **d.** to taking

4. Most college advisors tell new students that it will take time _____ to their new surroundings.

   a. adjusting   **b.** to adjust   **c.** to adjusting   **d.** adjust

5. As part of an exercise and diet program, one must stop _____ more calories than one burns.

   a. to consume   **b.** consuming   **c.** consume   **d.** to consuming

Error Correction   One of the five underlined words or phrases is not correct. Find the error and correct it. Be prepared to explain your answer.

6. <u>Taking</u> a public speaking course during the first semester of college <u>improves</u> [to]

   listening skills, <u>provides</u> practice in <u>organize</u> one's thoughts, and <u>builds</u> [organizing]

   self-confidence.

7. It <u>is</u> never a good idea <u>choose</u> a career <u>based</u> only on the money one <u>can earn</u>. [to]

   Similarly, one should avoid <u>making</u> a career decision before exploring several

   options.

8. Although <u>stay up</u> all night to <u>watch</u> movies <u>is</u> often typical of college students, this

   lifestyle tends <u>to change</u> once students begin <u>working</u> full time.

Egypt's Eman Gaber stretches during a fencing practice session before the start of the London 2012 Olympic Games.

ACTIVITY 9   **Building Greater Sentences**

Combine these short sentences into one sentence. You can add new words and move words around, but you should not add or omit any ideas. More than one answer is possible, but these sentences require gerund or infinitive forms.

1. a. Athletes stay physically fit.
   b. They do this by exercising every day.
   c. They do this by following a healthy diet.

_____

_____

2. a. Employers hire college graduates.
   b. These college graduates think independently and have good computer skills.
   c. Employers prefer these college graduates.
   d. A recent survey indicates this.

_____

_____

3. a. People can save the environment.
   b. People can save money.
   c. These require making small lifestyle changes.
   d. It is possible to do these things.

_____

_____

Steps to Composing

Read the paragraph about work–life balance. Then follow the instructions in the 10 steps to edit the information and composition of this paragraph. Write your revised paragraph on a separate sheet of paper. Be careful with capitalization and punctuation. Check your answers with the class.

PROCESS PARAGRAPH

Finding More Time

[1] Many people try to handle both personal and professional responsibilities, which is often an overwhelming task. [2] However, there are some simple steps people can take to put more time into their day. [3] The first step is to set realistic goals. [4] It is not realistic to have 15 items on a daily to-do list. [5] Instead, list the top three or four work items that need to be finished before the day is over. [6] Check off each item as it is accomplished. [7] The second step is scheduling all of one's personal activities, including exercise. [8] This means writing down what time one will go to the gym, take a walk, or practice yoga. [9] Doing this ensures some alone time will be available every day. [10] Finally, the last step is to learn to say "no" to people who waste one's time. [11] For example, instead of standing in the parking lot talking to a co-worker about the boss for 20 minutes, leave the office and head directly for home. [12] There is no easy solution to finding all the time one wants or needs, but if one takes these steps, it will lead one in the right direction.

---

1. In sentence 1, change the subject *Many people try* to *Trying*.

2. Because sentence 1 now begins with a gerund, omit *which* and the comma. The verb *is* now agrees with the subject *Trying*.

3. In sentence 2, replace *some* with the more specific term *three*.

4. Sentence 4 gives an example for sentence 3. Begin sentence 4 with *For example*.

5. In sentence 7, change the verb *is* to *requires*.

6. In sentence 9, change *alone* to the more academic term *private*.

7. In sentence 10, replace *to learn to say "no" to* with the more formal infinitive *to avoid*.

8. In sentence 12, change *if one takes* to *taking*.

9. In sentence 12, because the gerund is now the subject, omit the comma and the subject *it*.

10. In sentence 12, change *these steps* to the more specific *these three steps*.

ACTIVITY 11　**Original Writing**

On a separate sheet of paper, write a process paragraph (at least six sentences) about adjusting to a new situation or adapting to a new culture. Use at least one gerund and one infinitive and underline them; try to use more if possible.

Here are some examples of how to begin.

- *Moving to a new country often requires learning a new language and adjusting to new customs.*
- *Students who are in college for the first time need to follow three steps to adapt to the new responsibilities going to college brings.*
- *After finishing college, recent graduates who have found full-time jobs will need to adjust to their new lifestyle.*

Archduke Maximilian's study in Miramare Castle, Trieste, Italy, dates from the 19th century.

14

Writing with Noun Clauses

WHAT DO YOU KNOW?

DISCUSS Look at the photo and read the caption. Discuss the questions.

1. What is the most interesting feature of this room? Why is it interesting?

2. Think of a special room that you know, either in your own home or another place. What makes that room special?

FIND THE ERRORS This paragraph contains two errors with noun clauses. Find the errors and correct them. Explain your corrections to a partner.

NARRATIVE PARAGRAPH

The Mysterious Key

[1] Ben did not remember when he first saw the key. [2] It was a long, slender, silver key, and it had a faded red ribbon tied to it. [3] He did not tell anyone that he had found it in the center drawer of his grandfather's old oak desk. [4] He wondered what was the key for, so he walked from room to room in his grandparents' house, searching for a lock the key would open. [5] In his grandparents' bedroom, inside the nightstand next to the bed, Ben found a small wooden box. [6] The key fit! [7] What he found inside the box took his breath away. [8] He quickly locked the box, put it back into the nightstand, ran out of the bedroom, and placed the key back into the center drawer of his grandfather's desk. [9] Whether he ever told anyone was in the box also remains a mystery to this day.

Grammar Forms

14.1 Noun Clauses

A noun clause is a group of words that takes the place of a noun. It has a subject and verb and begins with *that*, a question word, or *if / whether*.

Type of Noun Clause	Example

1. *that* + subject + verb	NASA scientists have just announced **that** additional planets outside our
	                                                                                                S
	solar system have been discovered.
	                                    V

2. question word + subject + verb	**What** the researchers discovered changed the kind of treatments
	                   S V
	patients received.
	
	Many graduates do not know **where** they should apply for jobs after
	                                                          S V
	college.

3. *if / whether* + subject + verb	Environmentalists do not know **if** the damage to the lake is reversible.
	                                                     S V
	Whether a cure for all types of cancer will be found depends on funding.
	                    S V

Notes
1. Noun clause subjects take singular verbs.
   How often people change careers **is** the subject of a new university study.
2. *That*-clauses often come in sentences that start with *It is/was* + adjective.
   It is true **that** many businesses rely on repeat customers.
3. *That* is often omitted in *that*-clauses.
   Research indicates (that) sea levels have been rising at a rate of 0.14 inches per year since the early 1990s.
4. Noun clauses with question words or *if/whether* use statement word order (subject + verb).
   They are not sure **what** the data error is. (*Not*: They are not sure what is the data error.)

Underline the noun clauses in the following sentences.

1. In a recent nationwide poll, respondents stated whether they felt optimistic or pessimistic about a number of economic issues.

2. What defines a person's success varies from individual to individual.

3. Economic theory experts believe that increasing interest rates results in decreased consumer spending.

4. People commonly ask themselves if their work makes them happy.

5. Career counselors advise that who you know will help you find a job.

6. It is not surprising that so many people live to be 100 or older these days.

7. It is a fact that the media influences teens in several ways, including hair and clothing styles.

8. Many newly arrived immigrants do not know where they can find help with education and employment needs.

9. Advertisers who claim that their products can do everything from cure the common cold to promote excessive weight loss are often scrutinized by the Federal Trade Commission.

10. Studies show that small business owners who keep a list of priorities are more organized and successful than those who do not.

Common Uses

14.2 | Using Noun Clauses: Function

Noun clauses are commonly used in academic writing. They are used:

1. to express the ideas, theories, and discoveries of others	Jean Piaget, a Swiss psychologist, believed **that** the thinking process in children varied greatly from the thinking process in adults.
2. to paraphrase with reporting verbs	Recent studies show **that** people who give generously of their money are generally happier than those who do not.
3. to suggest or recommend something	Health experts recommend **that** adults get between seven and eight hours of sleep each night in order to maintain good health.

14.3 | Using Noun Clauses: Position

Noun clauses can go in different places in sentences. They are used:

1. as the subject of a sentence	Which career a person chooses tells a lot about his or her personality. Whether a business will succeed or fail depends on several critical factors.
2. as the object of a verb • Noun clauses are common after verbs that report what research shows, what people believe or think, or what someone has said.	Until 1897, doctors did not know how malaria parasites were transmitted. A recent survey of college seniors showed that many do not plan to attend graduate school.
3. as the object of a preposition **a.** with question words	Financial advisors receive training in how to help their clients save for retirement.
b. with *the fact, the idea,* or *the possibility + that*	Through labeling, consumers are informed about the fact that some products contain gluten, peanuts, and other potential allergens.
4. after *be* + certain adjectives	It is clear that many businesses rely on repeat customers to continue operating.

Notes

1. *The fact that, the idea that,* or *the belief that* are commonly used at the beginning of a sentence.
    The idea that global warming exists continues to be a topic of debate.
2. The word *that* after the reporting verb may be omitted in speaking and informal writing. However, it is usually included in academic writing.
    Researchers stated **that** more studies needed to be conducted on the drug's effectiveness.
3. Common verbs followed by noun clauses include *announce, ask, believe, claim, conclude, indicate, know, note, report, say, state, suggest,* and *think.*
4. Common adjectives followed by noun clauses include *aware, certain, clear, convinced, obvious, sure,* and *worried.*

ACTIVITY 2

Underline the correct word or phrase.

1. Medical researchers continue to study (*that / why*) some people live longer than others.

2. A recent survey showed (*if / that*) more students prefer reading their campus newspaper in print rather than online.

3. In their campaign speeches, candidates typically say (*that / what*) they think their audiences want to hear.

4. It is a fact (*that / which*) faculty at both liberal arts colleges and research universities conduct research and teach classes.

5. (*What / Whoever*) discovered the Faroe Islands remains unknown to this day.

6. Doctors have begun warning patients about (*that / the fact that*) overusing antibiotics can lead to antibiotic resistance and increased infections.

7. Although many citizens think (*what / that*) security cameras help prevent crime, there are reasons to limit their use.

8. The survey asked consumers (*which / that*) three things they wanted to know about the service at their local hospitals.

9. Researchers are investigating (*that / whether*) caffeine has positive health benefits.

10. (*Where / Why*) adults develop phobias is still largely unknown, but exposure therapy is a useful treatment for many sufferers.

Common Errors

Common Error 14.1   Is the word order correct?

they started
Participants in the survey were asked when ~~did they start~~ smoking.

immigrants can
Whether ~~can immigrants~~ become citizens depends on several factors.

REMEMBER: Use statement word order (subject + verb) in noun clauses that start with question words or *if / whether.*

ACTIVITY 3   **Common Error 14.1**

Read the following sentences. If the sentence is correct, write *C* on the line. If the sentence is incorrect, write *X* on the line. Then correct the sentence.

_____ **1.** A common concern among older citizens is how long will they be able to live alone.

_____ **2.** Due to conflicting results from different studies, doctors and nutritionists continue to debate whether are eggs good or bad for one's health.

_____ **3.** Why people wake up in an irritable mood is the subject of a new health study.

_____ **4.** Reading fiction allows the reader to discover what is the author's message.

_____ **5.** There are several ways to determine if a computer has a virus or not.

_____ **6.** Linguistic anthropologists continue to explore when did communication begin to evolve into language.

_____ **7.** As the number of electric cars increases, whether will pollution decrease remains to be seen.

_____ **8.** In the scientific method, formulating a hypothesis means stating what will be the results of the experiment.

Common Error 14.2   Is the verb form correct?

differs
How college advisors help students ~~differ~~ from one college to the next.

REMEMBER: Use a singular verb after a noun clause that is used as a subject.

Underline the noun clause in each sentence. If the verb form after the noun clause is correct, write *C* on the line. If it is incorrect, write *X* on the line. Then write the correct form above the verb.

_____ **1.** The fact that today's family structures are complex make the term *nuclear family* inadequate and outdated.

_____ **2.** What makes people change their thinking depends on the method used to present an opposing view.

_____ **3.** How colleges accommodate students with learning disabilities range from providing text-to-speech software to assigning classroom note takers.

_____ **4.** The fact that people abandon their pets causes animal shelters to become overcrowded.

_____ **5.** Whether capital punishment prevents crime has been the subject of many debates.

_____ **6.** How students prepare for exams vary from one individual to another.

Common Error 14.3   Is a question word or *that*-phrase missing?

what
Businesses want employees who believe in the company represents.
                                      ∧

the fact that
Some building contractors hide they are unlicensed.
                          ∧

REMEMBER: Include a question word or *that*-phrase after the verb (or verb + preposition) in a noun clause.

The following sentences are missing a question word or *that*-phrase. Put the word or phrase in parentheses in the correct place in the sentence. Change capitalization as needed.

1. Writers must clearly state the main point of the research paper is in the thesis statement. (*what*)

2. Schools can be classified according to they implement their curriculum and measure student performance. (*how*)

3. Geoscientists are interested in analyzing rock and soil samples may lead to predicting and even preventing future natural disasters. (*the idea that*)

4. One of the powers of the Supreme Court is to decide a law is constitutional or not. (*whether*)

5. Although scientists know the sun will die, it is impossible to know exactly it will happen. (*when*)

6. Salespeople do not always tell customers about there are problems with the product. (*the fact that*)

Common Error 14.4   Is the noun clause missing a subject or verb?

they
Whether would become famous was not the main force behind the musicians' motivation.
∧

was
Several health study participants said that keeping an exercise log harder than exercising.
∧

REMEMBER: Every noun clause requires a subject and a verb.

ACTIVITY 6   **Common Error 14.4**

Each noun clause in the sentences below is missing a subject or a verb. Underline the noun clause. Then add the missing subject or verb from the box.

a woman	construction	lead	talent
are	has	remains	they

1. How hard work and passion to success is the subject of numerous research studies.

2. The short story "The Yellow Wallpaper" depicts what experiences during a mental breakdown.

3. People like to believe that makes entrepreneurs successful rather than hard work.

4. Researchers are unsure why fewer people at risk for developing dementia today than there were 35 years ago.

5. From the beginning of the Golden Gate Bridge project in 1919, it was evident that would be an engineering challenge.

6. An increasingly common question asked of lawmakers about payday loans is if should be illegal.

7. Whether using visual imagery before a competition a positive result in an athlete's performance has been the focus of several psychological studies.

8. Investigators stated that the cause of ships and planes disappearing in the Bermuda Triangle unanswered to this day.

Academic Vocabulary

Verbs Frequently Used with Noun Clauses in Academic Writing

be	feel	prefer	report	show
do	find	remember	serve	suggest

Source: Corpus of Contemporary American English (Davies 2008–)

ACTIVITY 7 **Vocabulary in Academic Writing**

Complete the sentences with the correct form of the verbs listed in the box. For some sentences, more than one answer is possible.

Subject Area   **Example from Academic Writing**

Earth Science   **1.** As a result of advances in science, the average jewelry shopper is often unable to tell if a gemstone _____ natural or synthetic.

Psychology   **2.** What people _____ about an event often differs from what actually took place.

Education   **3.** Whether the test results _____ improved vocabulary development among students in bilingual programs remains unknown.

Technology   **4.** It is interesting that many people _____ to use their smartphones as computers rather than as phones.

History   **5.** According to historians, some accounts of war battles _____ that the greatest generals made decisions confidently and inspired their troops.

Business   **6.** Businesses generally gain repeat customers when people _____ the product they want at the price they want.

Political Science   **7.** Based on election day polls, it appears that senior citizens _____ more compelled to vote in an election than younger voters do.

Literature   **8.** What writers _____ is bring a reader's imagination alive.

Anthropology   **9.** Because of artifacts discovered near the Great Lakes, anthropologists have concluded that the area _____ as a Viking trading post.

Biology   **10.** What wildlife biologists _____ about animal behavior in the wild contributes to humanity's understanding of how a species survives.

Put It Together

Multiple Choice   Choose the letter of the correct answer.

1. _____ students choose as a major field of study often depends on advice they receive from their family, friends, advisor, and teachers.

   a. Whether   **b.** What   **c.** How   **d.** When

2. According to recent psychological studies, when people boast about their accomplishments, they are not always able to predict _____ others will react.

   a. what   **b.** why   **c.** the fact that   **d.** how

3. Although flying cars still seem like science fiction, _____ the Federal Aviation Authority (FAA) has given companies permission to build and test them.

   a. that   **b.** it is a fact that   **c.** if   **d.** whether or not

4. People who receive training in _____ to administer CPR (cardiopulmonary resuscitation) show increased willingness to help when someone has a heart attack.

   a. how   **b.** what   **c.** why   **d.** if

5. In 1873, a jury concluded _____ Susan B. Anthony was guilty of casting an illegal vote.

   a. what   **b.** when   **c.** if   **d.** that

Error Correction   One of the five underlined words or phrases is not correct. Find the error and correct it. Be prepared to explain your answer.

6. A group of college advisors is planning to study that setting goals affects students' study habits and whether setting specific goals results in a more successful semester.

7. In a recent study of runners and their heart health, researchers asked participants to record how often they ran, how far did they go, and what time of day they exercised.

8. Researchers report that whether people believe a politician's statements often depend on whether they support that candidate.

Women in Burkina Faso enjoy talking as they prepare flour.

ACTIVITY 9 **Building Greater Sentences**

Combine these short sentences into one sentence. You can add new words and move words around, but you should not add or omit any ideas. More than one answer is possible, but these sentences require noun clauses.

1. a. Aristotle observed something.
   b. Having a sense of purpose in life is connected to something.
   c. The connection is a feeling of happiness.

_____

_____

2. a. Exercise helps prevent certain types of diseases.
   b. Exercise does not help with weight loss.
   c. How this happens is the topic of a recent health study.

_____

_____

3. a. Sports experts had doubts.
   b. They doubted if anyone could beat a record.
   c. The record was the four-minute mile.
   d. This was in 1954.

_____

_____

Steps to Composing

Read the descriptive paragraph. Then follow the instructions in the 10 steps to edit the information and composition of this paragraph. Write your revised paragraph on a separate sheet of paper. Be careful with capitalization and punctuation. Check your answers with the class.

DESCRIPTIVE PARAGRAPH

Recognizing the Sleep-Deprived

¹ People who do not get enough sleep are said to be sleep-deprived. ² It is easy to identify people who are sleep-deprived by the way they look and the way they behave. ³ First of all, people who are sleep-deprived always look tired. ⁴ For example, their eyes are usually red or bloodshot, and they often have dark circles under their eyes. ⁵ Moreover, instead of the corners of their mouths turning up, the corners tend to droop, which makes them look sad. ⁶ People who are sleep-deprived are also easy to recognize by the impatient way they behave. ⁷ While waiting in line, they may tap their feet and mutter, "Come on. I don't have all day." ⁸ People who honk their car horns at the drivers in front of them as soon as the traffic light turns green are likely sleep-deprived. ⁹ In meetings, these people tap their pencils on the table and sigh heavily every few minutes. ¹⁰ Their struggle to stay awake is obvious. ¹¹ They yawn in the middle of important discussions. ¹² They put their heads down on their desks when they think no one is looking. ¹³ They are never without a cup of coffee in one hand and a snack in the other. ¹⁴ One keeps them awake, and one gives them energy. ¹⁵ These characteristics of people with chronic sleep deficiencies all point to one thing: people do not look or act their best when they do not get enough sleep.

---

1. In sentence 3, replace *people who are sleep-deprived* with *they* to avoid repetition.

2. In sentence 6, change *are sleep-deprived* again to *lack sleep* for variety.

3. In sentence 6, *the impatient way they behave* is awkward. Change it to *their impatient behavior.*

4. In sentence 8, replace *sleep-deprived* with *suffering from insufficient sleep* for variety.

5. In sentence 11, add *often* before *yawn* to avoid overgeneralizing.

6. Both sentences 11 and 12 give examples of behavior at work. Connect them with *and* and omit the second subject, *They.*

7. In sentence 13, replace the adverb *never* with *rarely* to avoid overgeneralizing.

8. In sentence 13, add the adjective *sugary* before *snack* for a more descriptive noun phrase.

9. In sentence 14, make the subjects more specific. Replace the first subject with *The coffee* and the second subject with *the sugary snack.*

10. In sentence 14, change *and* to *while* to emphasize the contrast between what is in each hand.

ACTIVITY 11 **Original Writing**

On a separate sheet of paper, write a descriptive paragraph (at least six sentences) describing a person, place, or thing. Use at least one noun clause and underline it; try to use at least two if possible.

Here are some examples of how to begin.

- *The characteristics of a positive learning environment include a sense of community, interesting lessons, and a respectful atmosphere.*
- *The ideal vacation spot has beautiful views, historic sites, and fantastic restaurants.*
- *A good manager has several characteristics.*

An Asian elephant walks among the giant trees of Havelock Island, India, in the Bay of Bengal.

15

Using Connectors for Better Writing

WHAT DO YOU KNOW?

DISCUSS Look at the photo and read the caption. Discuss the questions.

1. Describe a forest that is near where you live. What kinds of animals live there?

2. What types of trees are in your city or town? Are they green all year round?

FIND THE ERRORS This paragraph contains two errors with connectors. Find the errors and correct them. Explain your corrections to a partner.

CLASSIFICATION PARAGRAPH

Forest Biomes

¹A biome is a large area that has a similar climate and similar plants and animals. ²Biomes can be categorized in different ways including, for example, deserts, coral reefs, grasslands, and forests. ³Within a biome category, there may also be smaller groups or divisions. ⁴The forest biome is such an example. ⁵Within the forest biome, there are different types of forests and different kinds of trees. ⁶However, a deciduous forest contains trees that lose their leaves in the fall and grow new ones in the spring. ⁷A maple tree is an example of a deciduous tree. ⁸In contrast, a coniferous forest contains trees that have needle-like leaves. ⁹These coniferous trees are green all year round, or they are sometimes called *evergreen* trees. ¹⁰A pine tree is an example of a coniferous tree. ¹¹A forest that has both deciduous and coniferous trees is called a mixed forest.

Grammar Forms

15.1 | Connectors

Connectors	Example

1. Coordinating conjunctions
   a. Coordinating conjunctions connect words or phrases. They also connect independent clauses in compound sentences.
   b. Common coordinating conjunctions include *and, but, or,* and *so.*
	Some new businesses advertise on social media, **but** others prefer to advertise on television and radio.

2. Subordinating conjunctions
   a. Subordinating conjunctions connect dependent clauses with independent clauses in complex sentences.
   b. Common subordinating conjunctions include *after, although, because, before, when,* and *while.*
	Although the cost of a college education is high, the benefits outweigh the cost.

3. Transitions
   a. Transitions connect related ideas between sentences and/or paragraphs.
   b. Common transitions include *also, as a result, finally, first, however, in addition, in contrast, next, second, then,* and *therefore.*
	Occupational therapists help patients improve their daily life skills. **In addition,** they may recommend special equipment for patients.

15.2 | Punctuation with Connectors

Pattern	Example
1. Coordinating conjunctions Use a comma before the conjunction joining two independent clauses	Many people use antibacterial soap to prevent illness**, but** some health officials believe plain soap works just as well.

2. Subordinating conjunctions
   a. Use a comma when the dependent clause comes first.
   b. Do not use a comma when the independent clause comes first.
	Although it may lower future health-care costs**,** many people postpone having an annual physical.
	
	 Many people postpone having an annual physical **although** it may lower future health-care costs.

3. Transitions

a. Use a period (or semi-colon) before a transition and a comma after the transition.	Many consumers receive dozens of telemarketing calls daily. **As a result**, the government has established a registry to stop unwanted calls.

b. Use a comma:
  i. before and after the transition when it comes between a subject and verb
  ii. before the transition when it is at the end of the sentence
	Many consumers receive dozens of telemarketing calls daily; **as a result**, the government has established a registry to stop unwanted calls.
	
	Some people exercise to lower stress; others, **however**, prefer to use diet to reduce stress.
	
	Some people exercise to lower stress; others prefer to use diet to reduce stress, **however**.

Notes
1. A comma is not used after the transition *then*.
2. Commas are also used to connect three or more similar items. A comma is not used to connect two similar items.
   Three endangered species are the black rhino, the mountain gorilla, **and** the Sumatran tiger.
   Two endangered species are the black rhino **and** the mountain gorilla.

ACTIVITY 1

Read each sentence. Write *CC* over coordinating conjunctions, *SC* over subordinating conjunctions, and *T* over transitions.

1. Before the mid-1800s, people colored their hair with natural dyes, but an English chemist changed the world of hair color when he created a permanent dye using coal tar.

2. Many consumers mistakenly believe that all organically grown food is the same; however, there are differences. Some foods are considered organic, while others are considered 100 percent organic.

3. In the past, a subculture might include hippies, while today, a subculture might include gamers, people who play interactive video games, for example.

4. Because schools have begun to incorporate technology into classroom learning, children are becoming independent learners, learning at their own pace, and developing real-world skills.

5. During a jury trial, attorneys for both sides present evidence and call witnesses to testify. Next, the jury considers the evidence and reaches a verdict of guilty or not guilty. Finally, depending on the verdict, the judge either releases or sentences the defendant.

6. A recent study showed that consumers enjoyed the ease and convenience of online shopping, but it also showed that they hated the pop-up ads that cluttered their screens.

7. Although some people might consider Plato the father of Western philosophy, there are several reasons why Socrates should have this title.

8. In the 1800s, the east coast of the United States began to get crowded, so many pioneers began migrating west in order to buy land, find better jobs, or search for gold.

Read the sentences. Write *C* if the punctuation is correct and *X* if it is wrong. Then correct the incorrect punctuation.

_____ **1.** Courses in the humanities include art, literature, philosophy, and history.

_____ **2.** Logging of rainforests continues, although governments are aware of how deforestation affects the environment.

_____ **3.** Research shows an increase in the number of colleges encouraging the use of e-books, however, many students still prefer to read hardcover textbooks.

_____ **4.** Before becoming President of the United States. Theodore Roosevelt held numerous political positions, including that of governor of New York.

_____ **5.** Some very ill patients enroll in clinical trials, because they want to contribute to science.

_____ **6.** Students who cram for tests are often able to remember enough to pass them. Then, they forget what they studied because they have not really learned it.

_____ **7.** One advantage of attending a community college is the low-cost tuition. In addition, class sizes in a community college are generally smaller than in a four-year institution.

_____ **8.** Children growing up 50 years ago commonly played with toys and read books, in contrast, many of today's children play video games and read stories on tablets or e-readers.

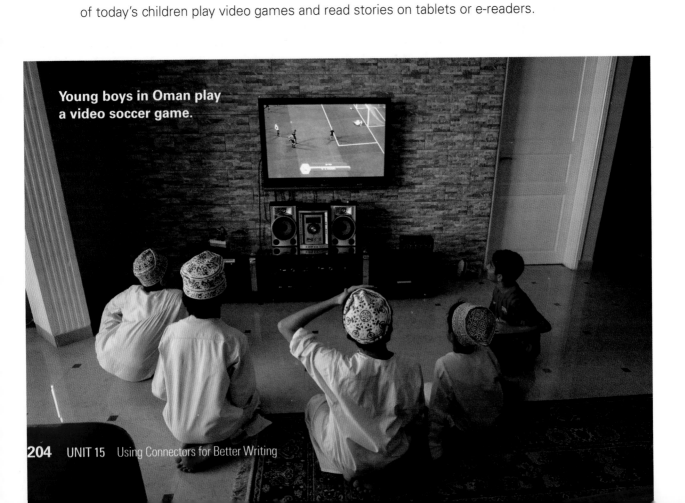

Young boys in Oman play a video soccer game.

Common Uses

15.3 Using Coordinating Conjunctions

Coordinating conjunctions show the relationship between words, phrases, or sentences. They are used:

1. to show addition (*and*)	Plants need air, water, sun, **and** nutrients to survive.
2. to show contrast (*but, yet*)	Abraham Lincoln's Gettysburg Address was a short **but** powerful speech.
3. to show choice (*or*)	The most popular cruises are to the Caribbean **or** to Alaska.
4. to show result (*so*)	During a recession, unemployment rises, **so** consumers try to save more and spend less.

15.4 Using Subordinating Conjunctions

Subordinating conjunctions show the relationship between a dependent clause and an independent clause. They are used:

1. to show contrast (*although, even though, while*)	**Although** the cost of a college education is high, the benefits outweigh the cost.
2. to show reason (*as, because, since*)	Protecting one's personal information is important **because** identity theft continues to grow.
3. to show time (*after, as soon as, before, until, when, while*)	A good test-taking strategy is to preview the entire test **before** answering any questions on it.

Transitions connect related ideas between independent clauses (sentences) or paragraphs. They show:

1. addition (*in addition, also, furthermore*)	A person found guilty of a crime may be sentenced to prison. **In addition**, the person may be required to pay a fine.
2. contrast (*however, in contrast*)	Cell phones allow users to communicate anytime and anywhere; **however**, their use often results in less face-to-face interaction.
3. result (*therefore, as a result, consequently, thus*)	A person's career may span over 40 years. **Therefore**, it is important to find a meaningful career.
4. examples (*for example, for instance*)	A short story includes several literary elements. **For example**, it has characters, a setting, a theme, and a plot.
5. sequence (*first, next, then, finally, last*)	There are several ways to pay for college. **First**, apply for available scholarships and grants. **Next**, look into getting a private loan.

ACTIVITY 3

For each sentence, underline the correct connector to show the relationship given in parentheses. Use the punctuation in the sentence to help you choose the connector.

1. There are several rhetorical styles used in academic writing. (*For example / However / As a result*), descriptive writing uses details involving the five senses—sight, taste, smell, touch, and hearing—to create a picture in the reader's mind. (example)

2. A career in aerospace engineering pays well, (*although / but / however*) job opportunities are projected to decrease over the next decade for a number of reasons. (contrast)

3. In some cultures, women are viewed as delicate and fragile, (*as a result / so / therefore*) their participation in sports such as soccer or kickboxing may be viewed negatively. (result)

4. (*Until / When / Before*) natural disasters occur, several worldwide agencies work together to provide food, water, shelter, and medical care to victims. (time)

5. During difficult economic times, people often look for a sign of hope. The racehorse Seabiscuit was that sign during the Depression (*so / then / because*) the small underrated horse won race after race and became a champion. (reason)

6. Every culture has legends, which explain its customs or its heroes. (*And / For example / In addition*), every culture has folktales, which have a moral, and often teach appropriate behavior. (addition)

Common Errors

Common Error 15.1   Is there an extra connector?

Although people may agree that texting while driving is dangerous, ~~but~~ they cannot agree on how to prevent it.

People
~~Although people~~ may agree that texting while driving is dangerous, but they cannot agree on how to prevent it.

REMEMBER: Use either a subordinating conjunction or a coordinating conjunction to connect a dependent clause with an independent clause. Do not use both.

ACTIVITY 4   **Common Error 15.1**

Each sentence or pair of sentences below contains an unnecessary connector. Cross out the extra connector, and make any capitalization or punctuation changes needed. There may be more than one way to correct a sentence.

1. Citizens participate in local government by electing city officials. Furthermore, citizens also have the opportunity to share their views and opinions at city council meetings.

2. While sugar-free foods may help people lose weight, but they may also lead people to eat more because they think they have "saved" calories.

3. Although many may think *Hamlet* is Shakespeare's most popular play, yet *Romeo and Juliet* is, in fact, the most popular one.

4. Because the honeybee population has steadily declined and bee colonies have collapsed, so the U.S. Department of Agriculture has taken steps to identify the causes and find a solution.

5. Although researchers have not yet found a cure for HIV, but they are hopeful they will be close to a cure within the next five years.

6. Because melanoma is one of the most dangerous types of skin cancer, so people need to avoid the sun during the hottest time of the day, wear sunscreen, and see a dermatologist every year.

7. Although researchers have identified the genes that allow lizards to regrow their tails, but they are in the beginning stages of applying their knowledge in ways to help people.

8. The decision to start a business is not an easy one to make. Consequently, to make the right decision, an entrepreneur must, therefore, make the commitment to raise capital, set goals, and work hard.

Common Error 15.2   Is the connector correct?

Surveys show that most college graduates owe an average of $35,000 in student loans when

because

they graduate; therefore, tuition and fees continue to rise.

REMEMBER: Use the connector that shows the correct relationship.

ACTIVITY 5   **Common Error 15.2**

Underline the connectors in each sentence. If all the connectors are correct, write *C* on the line. If any connectors are wrong, write *X* on the line. Then write the correct connector(s) above the sentence. More than one answer may be possible.

_____ **1.** When robotic surgery offers several advantages to the patient and the surgeon, the cost of the system is extremely expensive.

_____ **2.** Newton was not hit on the head by a falling apple, and it was a falling apple that led him to develop his law of gravity and later write about this principle.

_____ **3.** Many students change their career paths but they take college classes. A professor may inspire them, for example, to consider a new field.

_____ **4.** An example of self-motivating behavior is making New Year's resolutions. People often resolve to exercise daily although they want to lose weight.

_____ **5.** People enroll in college for a variety of reasons. Some enroll because they enjoy learning, while others enroll to earn a degree and begin a career.

_____ **6.** If the president of the United States is unable to perform the duties of the office, the line of succession begins with the vice president, then moves to the Speaker of the House of Representatives, is followed by the president pro tempore of the Senate, and next, is followed by cabinet members.

_____ **7.** Type 1 diabetes cannot be prevented and often starts in early childhood; in addition, type 2 diabetes can be prevented by eating healthy food or exercising.

_____ **8.** There are two factors that contribute to changes in an ecosystem. First, there are direct factors. For example, climate change and pollution are direct factors.

Common Error 15.3 Is a connector missing?

but
Many people immigrate for political reasons, others immigrate for economic reasons.
^

REMEMBER: Use a connector (a coordinating conjunction, a subordinating conjunction, or a transition) to join clauses and show relationships between clauses.

ACTIVITY 6 **Common Error 15.3**

For each sentence, fill in the blank with the correct connector. Use the punctuation in the sentence to help you. For some sentences, more than one answer may be possible.

1. College libraries offer many valuable services online, _____ many students are unaware of these resources.

2. In 1955, _____ Rosa Parks was arrested for not giving up her seat on the bus to a white man, African-Americans boycotted the Montgomery, Alabama, bus system for over a year.

3. Many Native American languages are becoming extinct. _____, one Native American tribe, the Ojibwe, has created podcasts of language lessons to encourage young tribal members to learn and retain the language.

4. Most experts recommend smartphone users leave their phones on _____ they have finished using them.

5. Allergists offer helpful advice to people who suffer when pollen counts are high. _____, they suggest keeping windows and doors closed and using the car air conditioner while driving.

6. A recent survey showed that most adults consider it acceptable to use a cell phone while walking outside. _____, only a small number consider it acceptable to do so during a meeting.

7. _____ the teaching profession does not pay as well as other professions, schools are facing teacher shortages.

8. Students who enroll in a culinary arts school learn the techniques and theories of cooking, _____ they often learn hotel and restaurant management skills as well.

Common Error 15.4   Is punctuation missing or incorrect?

age
People are retiring at an older ~~age,~~ because they need the money.

Studies show learning a foreign language as a child results in near-native pronunciation ˄in contrast, learning a foreign language as an adult does not. [;]

The gray wolf was once endangered ˄but its population is now stable. [,]

REMEMBER: • Do not use a comma with subordinating conjunctions when the independent clause is before the dependent clause.
   • A semi-colon can be used before a transition.
   • Use a comma before a coordinating conjunction when connecting two independent clauses.
   • Use a comma after the transition when two independent clauses form one sentence.

ACTIVITY 7   **Common Error 15.4**

Find and correct the punctuation error in each sentence or group of sentences. Make any capitalization changes needed. More than one answer may be possible.

1. Although Pierre-Auguste Renoir, the French impressionist painter, had severe arthritis he continued to paint until his death in 1919.

2. In 1988, the United Nations peacekeepers received the Nobel Peace Prize for their efforts as a result they gained the trust of many nations.

3. Classroom teachers may take one of two approaches in the classroom. One is to encourage cooperative behavior, in which students work together to meet a goal or objective, in contrast, encouraging competitive behavior is an approach in which students work alone and may even compete against each other for grades.

4. While foreign particles in the atmosphere are not necessary for a blue sky they are needed for the deep red sunrises and sunsets people enjoy.

5. Critical thinkers distinguish fact from opinion. For example, "Ottawa is the capital of Canada" is a fact but "Ottawa is the best place to go on vacation" is an opinion.

6. Although, many businesses offer health benefits to their employees, some large employers have reduced their employees' hours to avoid having to offer benefits.

7. Earth and Mars are two very different planets, but they still share some similarities. Both planets have days that are about 24 hours long, in addition, both planets have seasons and similar axis tilts.

8. Each country has a favorite national or regional dish, one which is made with local ingredients and which reflects the country's culture. For example Hungary is known for its goulash, Spain for its paella, and Saudi Arabia for its Kabsa.

Academic Vocabulary

Verbs Frequently Used with Connectors in Academic Writing

be	do	make	should	suggest
can	have	recognize	state	take

Source: Corpus of Contemporary American English (Davies 2008–)

ACTIVITY 8   **Vocabulary in Academic Writing**

Complete the sentences with the correct form of the correct verb in parentheses.

Subject Area	Example from Academic Writing
History	**1.** Historians often disagree about the causes of war, but all historians _____ (*recognize / suggest / have*) its impact on a nation.
Business	**2.** Companies _____ (*do / take / make*) every effort to test market a product. In addition, they conduct studies to identify potential users of the product.
Health	**3.** Although most participants in the health study agreed that they _____ (*should / do / have*) exercise more, few changed their habits.
Psychology	**4.** Initial research showed that parents do not _____ (*be / make / take*) their children to psychologists because they do not believe it will help.
Education	**5.** While many children enter school intellectually prepared to learn, some _____ (*have / state / be*) still in need of basic social skills.
Political Science	**6.** State governments are modeled after the federal government, so they _____ (*state / have / should*) the same three branches.
Environmental Science	**7.** Environmental scientists recently _____ (*state / recognize / make*) to Congress that the nation's air quality is continuing to decline rapidly.
Literature	**8.** In "The Interlopers," the narrator appeals to the reader's emotions with specific events. For example, the narrator _____ (*make / can / suggest*) that the two characters will become friends, causing the reader to feel their joy.
Philosophy	**9.** Studying philosophy _____ (*be / can / take*) help one become better at using logic to evaluate and solve problems.
Music	**10.** Listening to classical music while studying _____ (*be / should / do*) not guarantee a student will perform better on an exam.

Put It Together

ACTIVITY 9   Review Quiz

Multiple Choice   Choose the letter of the correct answer.

1. When asked what they would try if they knew they could not fail, many survey respondents said they would quit their jobs. _____ they said they would start their own businesses.

   a. In contrast,   **b.** And   **c.** However,   **d.** In addition,

2. According to a Federal Reserve Board survey, about 47 percent of respondents would either borrow money _____ they would sell something if they needed $400 for an emergency.

   a. or   **b.** and   **c.** next,   **d.** , also

3. _____ many electronic devices consume energy 24 hours a day, consumers should unplug their devices whenever they are not being used.

   a. After   **b.** While   **c.** Because   **d.** Although

4. Research indicates that approximately 40 percent of adults have been on a cruise and another 40 percent plan to go on one. _____ 20 percent of adults say they will never go on a cruise.

   a. In addition,   **b.** In contrast,   **c.** Although   **d.** Therefore,

5. President Theodore Roosevelt designated public land as national forests and established wildlife refuges. _____ Roosevelt is often referred to as "the conservationist president."

   a. Because   **b.** As a result,   **c.** In addition,   **d.** In contrast,

Error Correction   One of the five underlined words or phrases is not correct. Find the error and correct it. Be prepared to explain your answer.

6. Because they commonly live among the people while they are studying them, anthropologists can observe people's habits and traits. However, they can identify which habits are common and which habits are not.

7. Working for a relief organization offers the opportunity to save lives and change the future, because it also requires patience and physical stamina. As a result, before accepting a position with a relief organization, preparation is essential.

8. Consumers can order most things online, including, for example, food or prescriptions. Therefore, ordering prescriptions online may save time and money, there are risks. When an online pharmacy has no contact information, it is probably unreliable.

ACTIVITY 10   Building Greater Sentences

Combine these short sentences into one sentence. You can add new words and move words around, but you should not add or omit any ideas. More than one answer is possible, but all of these sentences require connectors.

1. a. Introverts need to be alone to recover their energy.
   b. Extroverts need stimulation in order to feel energized.
   c. Extroverts need the stimulation of being around other people.
   d. This is in contrast to introverts.

_____

_____

2. a. Globalization has made people aware of other cultures.
   b. It is unlikely that all cultures will merge.
   c. It is unlikely that all cultures will become one world culture.

_____

_____

3. a. Exams contain instructions.
   b. There may be several different types of instructions on an exam.
   c. It is important to read exam instructions carefully.

_____

_____

Read the comparison paragraph about foreign language learning. Then follow the directions in the 10 steps to edit the information and composition of this paragraph. Write your revised paragraph on a separate sheet of paper. Be careful with capitalization and punctuation. Check your answers with the class.

COMPARISON PARAGRAPH

How Learning a Foreign Language Has Changed

[1] Learning a foreign language today is different from learning one 25 years ago. [2] One difference is in the methods. [3] Today, students practice all four skills: listening, speaking, reading, and writing. [4] They work with partners to share and compare answers, and they have small group discussions. [5] In the past, students spent much of their class time studying grammar. [6] They worked alone and waited for their instructor to give them the answers. [7] Their speaking practice focused on repeating grammar drills or memorized conversations. [8] Another difference in learning a foreign language is in the materials. [9] Classroom materials include books with reading, writing, speaking, and listening activities. [10] Technology allows students to watch and listen to videos and then discuss them. [11] Twenty-five years ago, classroom materials were grammar books filled with drills and no reading or writing activities. [12] Learning a foreign language today is much more interactive and engaging for the student.

1. In sentence 1, replace *is different* with the active verb *differs.*

2. In sentence 2, add the adjective *noticeable* to emphasize the difference.

3. In sentence 4, begin the sentence with the transition *In addition* and a comma.

4. In sentence 4, add the adverb *collaboratively* after the verb *work.*

5. In sentence 5, add the transition *however* and a comma before the subject to emphasize the contrast between methods.

6. Begin sentence 9 with *For example* and a comma.

7. Begin sentence 10 with *Today* and a comma.

8. Begin sentence 11 with *In contrast* and a comma.

9. In sentence 11, change *and* to *but* to emphasize contrast.

10. In sentence 12, add *both the instructor and* between *for* and *the student* to emphasize that the teacher is also affected.

ACTIVITY 12   **Original Writing**

On a separate sheet of paper, write a comparison paragraph (at least six sentences). Compare two people, places, or things. Use connectors in your paragraph.

Here are some examples of how to begin.

- *College instructors are different from high school teachers in several important ways.*
- *Learning another language is similar to learning to play a musical instrument.*
- *Laptops and tablets have several things in common.*

APPENDIX 1   Building Greater Sentences

Being a good writer involves many skills, such as being able to write with correct grammar, vary your vocabulary, and state ideas concisely. A good writer also learns to create longer, more detailed sentences from simple ideas. Study the short sentences below.

Jim Thorpe won two medals.

The medals were Olympic medals.

They were gold medals.

He won them in 1912.

He was not allowed to keep the medals.

Notice that every sentence has an important piece of information. A good writer would not write all these sentences separately. Instead, the most important information from each sentence can be used to create one longer, coherent sentence.

Read the sentences again; this time, the important information has been circled.

(Jim Thorpe) won (two medals.)

The medals were (Olympic) medals.

They were (gold) medals.

He won them (in 1912.)

He was (not allowed to keep) the medals.

Here are some strategies for taking the circled information and creating a new sentence.

1. Create time phrases to introduce or end a sentence: in 1912
2. Find the key nouns: Jim Thorpe, medals
3. Find key adjectives: two, Olympic, gold
4. Create noun phrases: two + Olympic + gold + medals
5. Connect main ideas with conjunctions: won medals + but not allowed to keep them

Now read this improved, longer sentence:

In 1912, Jim Thorpe won two Olympic gold medals, but he was not allowed to keep them.

Here are some additional strategies for building better sentences.

1. Use coordinating conjunctions (*and, but, or, nor, yet, for, so*) to connect related ideas equally.
2. Use subordinating conjunctions, such as *after, while, since,* and *because* to connect related ideas when one idea is more important than the other.
3. Use clauses with relative pronouns, such as *who, which, that,* and *whose* to describe or define a noun or noun phrase.
4. Use pronouns to refer to previously mentioned information.

Part of Speech	Definition	Example
Adjective	An adjective is a word that describes a noun or pronoun.	Hurricane winds can be extremely **destructive**.
Adverb	An adverb is a word that describes a verb, an adjective, or another adverb.	Before starting any experiment, chemists must **carefully** prepare the chemicals involved.
Article	The definite article *the* is used with specific nouns. The indefinite articles *a* and *an* are used with singular count nouns.	**The** cottonmouth is **an** example of **a** poisonous snake.
Auxiliary	An auxiliary is a helping verb that is used with a main verb. Common auxiliaries are *be, do, have, will,* and modals such as *may, should,* and *could.*	Voters **did** not pass the new law, but supporters **may** try to write a different law.
Conjunction	A conjunction is used to connect words, phrases, or clauses. A coordinating conjunction connects two independent clauses. Common conjunctions are *and, but,* and *so.*	The capital of the United States used to be Philadelphia, **but** now it is Washington, D.C.
Noun	A noun is a person, place, thing, or idea. A noun can be used as an adjective.	The **Bengal tiger** has been listed as an endangered species since 2010.
Object	An object is a word that comes after a transitive (action) verb or a preposition.	Thomas Jefferson signed the **Declaration of Independence** in 1776.
Preposition	A preposition is a word that shows relationships between nouns, such as location, time, or direction. Prepositions can consist of one, two, or three words.	The books **about** gravity are located **in** the physics section **of** the library, **behind** the biology section.
Stative verb	Stative (nonactive) verbs describe states, senses, feelings, appearance, desires, or possession. Stative verbs are not usually used with progressive forms.	Early astronomers **believed** that Earth was the center of our universe.
Subject	The subject of a sentence tells who or what the sentence is about.	The **professor** is absent this term because he is on a sabbatical leave.
Verb	A verb shows the action of a sentence or the existence of something.	The people of Brazil **speak** Portuguese.

APPENDIX 3 Capitalization and Punctuation

Basic Capitalization

Rule	Example
Always capitalize the first word of a sentence.	**T**oday the board members will meet to discuss the new zoning laws.
Always capitalize the word *I* no matter where it is in a sentence.	Although **I** have carefully planned, **I** realize that there are risks in the experiment.
Capitalize proper nouns—the names of specific people, places, or things. Capitalize a person's title, including *Mr.*, *Mrs.*, *Ms.*, and *Dr.*	**D**r. **S**mith teaches sociology with her colleague **M**s. **W**ong.
Capitalize names of countries and other geographic areas. Capitalize the names of people from those areas. Capitalize the names of languages.	The official language of **C**hina is **S**tandard **C**hinese, or **M**andarin. However, **C**hinese people speak many different language varieties and dialects.
Capitalize titles of works, such as books, movies, and pieces of art.	Art historians have been analyzing the *Mona Lisa* to learn about its history and the painting techniques used.

Geographic Names

Rule	Example
Use *the* with countries that look plural or have the word *United*, *Republic*, or *Kingdom*.	the Netherlands the Philippines the United States the United Kingdom the former Soviet Union the Kingdom of Saudi Arabia
Use *the* with deserts, forests, mountain ranges, and certain other geographic areas.	the Sahara Desert the Amazon Rain Forest the Middle East (*but* Southeast Asia) the Pacific Northwest the South
Use *the* with most bodies of water, except individual lakes.	the Nile River the Mississippi River the Atlantic Ocean the Mediterranean Sea the Great Lakes (*but* Lake Erie)

End Punctuation

Rule	Example
Period (.) A period is used at the end of a declarative sentence.	The Battle of Agincourt was fought in France in October of 1415**.**
Question mark (?) A question mark is used at the end of a question.	Which country gave the Statue of Liberty to the United States**?**
Exclamation point (!) An exclamation point is used at the end of an exclamation. It is very rarely used in academic writing.	The research team finally captured the giant squid on film**!**

Commas

Rule	Example
A comma separates the items in a list of three or more things. There should be a comma between each item in the list.	She speaks French**,** English**,** and Chinese.
A comma separates two independent clauses when there is a coordinating conjunction such as *and, but, or, so, for, nor,* and *yet.*	Students can register for classes in person**,** or they may submit their applications by mail.
A comma is used to separate an introductory word or phrase from the rest of the sentence.	In conclusion**,** doctors are advising people to make sure they exercise at least 20 minutes a day.
A comma is used to separate an appositive from the rest of the sentence. An appositive is a word or group of words that renames a noun before it and provides additional information about the noun.	Washington**,** <u>the first president of the United States</u>**,** was a clever military leader.
A comma is sometimes used with adjective clauses. An adjective clause usually begins with a relative pronoun (*who, that, which, whom, whose, whoever,* or *whomever*). Use a comma when the information in the clause is unnecessary or extra. (This is also called a nonrestrictive clause.)	*A Brief History of Time*, which was written by Steven Hawking, is an introduction to physics for readers new to the subject.

APPENDIX 4   Irregular Verbs

Base Form	Simple Past	Past Participle
be	was, were	been
beat	beat	beaten
become	became	become
begin	began	begun
bend	bent	bent
bite	bit	bitten
blow	blew	blown
break	broke	broken
bring	brought	brought
build	built	built
buy	bought	bought
catch	caught	caught
choose	chose	chosen
come	came	come
cost	cost	cost
cut	cut	cut
dig	dug	dug
dive	dived, dove	dived
do	did	done
draw	drew	drawn
drink	drank	drunk
drive	drove	driven
eat	ate	eaten
fall	fell	fallen
feed	fed	fed
feel	felt	felt
fight	fought	fought
find	found	found
fit	fit	fit, fitted
fly	flew	flown
forget	forgot	forgotten
forgive	forgave	forgiven
freeze	froze	frozen
get	got	got, gotten
give	gave	given
go	went	gone
grow	grew	grown
hang	hung	hung
have	had	had
hear	heard	heard
hide	hid	hidden
hit	hit	hit
hold	hid	hidden
hurt	hurt	hurt
keep	kept	kept
know	knew	known
lay	laid	laid

Base Form	Simple Past	Past Participle
light	lit, lighted	lit, lighted
lose	lost	lost
make	made	made
mean	meant	meant
meet	met	met
pay	paid	paid
prove	proved	proved, proven
put	put	put
quit	quit	quit
read	read	read
ride	rode	ridden
ring	rang	rung
rise	rose	risen
run	ran	run
say	said	said
seek	sought	sought
sit	sat	sat
sleep	slept	slept
slide	slid	slid
speak	spoke	spoken
spend	spent	spent
spread	spread	spread
stand	stood	stood
steal	stole	stolen
stick	stuck	stuck
strike	struck	struck
swear	swore	sworn
sweep	swept	swept
swim	swam	swum
take	took	taken
teach	taught	taught
tear	tore	torn
tell	told	told
think	thought	thought
throw	threw	thrown
understand	understood	understood
upset	upset	upset
wake	woke	woken
wear	wore	worn
win	won	won
write	wrote	written

Prepositions

Single

			### Multi-word
about	between	onto	according to
above	beyond	opposite	because of
across	by	out	due to
against	down	outside	in back/front of
along	during	over	in place of
among	for	since	in spite of
around	from	through	instead of
as	in	throughout	next to
at	inside	toward(s)	with regard to
before	into	underneath	
behind	near	until	
below	of	up	
beneath	off	upon	
beside	on	with	
		within	
		without	

Preposition Combinations

Verb + Preposition

account for	differ from	look for / at	talk about
agree with	focus on	participate in	wait for
depend on	listen to	result in	worry about

Adjective + Preposition

afraid of	consistent with	interested in	similar to
associated with	different from	necessary for	tired of
aware of	familiar with	ready for	worried about
capable of	famous for	related to	
compared to / with	important for	satisfied with	

Noun + Preposition

the cause of	the example of	the need for	the reason for
the development of	the increase in	the number of	the relationship between
the difference between	the lack of	the percent of	

Sentence Fragments

Definition	Solution
A sentence fragment is a group of words that is not a complete sentence. A fragment is usually missing either a subject or a verb, or it is a dependent clause. A dependent clause is never a complete sentence. To correct a sentence fragment: • add a subject or verb, *or* • combine two clauses	**Add a subject.** ✗ A fungus is not an animal. Is an organism belonging to a group called *Fungi*. ✓ A fungus is not an animal. **It** is an organism belonging to a group called *Fungi*. **Combine two clauses.** ✗ Charles Darwin traveled to the Galapagos Islands. Because he wanted to study the unique creatures. ✓ Charles Darwin traveled to the Galapagos Islands **because** he wanted to study the unique creatures.

Run-on Sentences

Definition	Solution
A run-on sentence is two sentences incorrectly joined without a comma and coordinating conjunction (*and, but,* or *so*). To correct a run-on sentence: • add a comma and a connecting word, *or* • add a period to separate the sentence into two sentences	**Separate into two sentences.** ✗ The three branches of the United States government are the Executive, the Legislative, and the Judicial branches the president is part of the Executive branch. ✓ The three branches of the United States government are the Executive, the Legislative, and the Judicial branches**.** **T**he president is part of the Executive branch.

Comma Splices

Definition	Solution
A comma splice occurs when two or more sentences or independent clauses are connected with a comma. To correct a comma splice: • add a connecting word after the comma, • create two sentences from the one, *or* • combine the most important words into one sentence and add a subordinating conjunction (*because, since, although*)	**Add a connecting word.** ✗ Michelangelo created his statue *David* in 1504, it is considered a masterpiece of Renaissance sculpture. ✓ Michelangelo created his statue *David* in 1504, **and** it is considered a masterpiece of Renaissance sculpture. **Create two sentences.** ✓ Michelangelo created his statue *David* in 1504**.** **It** is considered a masterpiece of Renaissance sculpture. **Add a subordinating conjunction.** ✗ Astronauts usually stay on the International Space Station for only four to six months, being in zero gravity is hard on the human body. ✓ **Because** being in zero gravity is hard on the human body, astronauts usually stay on the International Space Station for only four to six months.

A paragraph is a group of sentences about one topic or one idea. It may have a title at the top. The first sentence of the paragraph is indented. The topic sentence is often near the beginning and introduces the main idea. The sentences in the body of the paragraph are connected to the topic sentence. They support and build on the main idea with facts, details, and reasons. The concluding sentence usually states the main point again or summarizes the main idea of the paragraph.

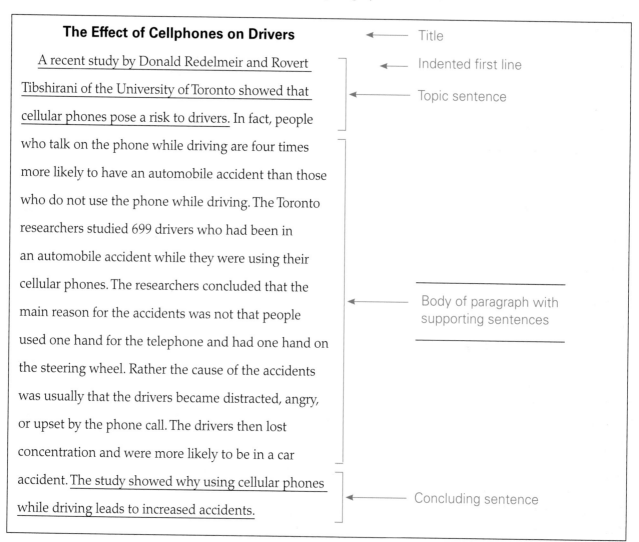

The Effect of Cellphones on Drivers ← Title

    A recent study by Donald Redelmeir and Rovert Tibshirani of the University of Toronto showed that cellular phones pose a risk to drivers. ← Indented first line / Topic sentence

In fact, people who talk on the phone while driving are four times more likely to have an automobile accident than those who do not use the phone while driving. The Toronto researchers studied 699 drivers who had been in an automobile accident while they were using their cellular phones. The researchers concluded that the main reason for the accidents was not that people used one hand for the telephone and had one hand on the steering wheel. Rather the cause of the accidents was usually that the drivers became distracted, angry, or upset by the phone call. The drivers then lost concentration and were more likely to be in a car accident. ← Body of paragraph with supporting sentences

The study showed why using cellular phones while driving leads to increased accidents. ← Concluding sentence

	Coordinating Conjunctions (connect independent clauses)	Subordinating Conjunctions (begin dependent clauses)	Transitions (usually precede independent clauses)
Examples			For example, In particular, Specifically, To illustrate,
Information	and		Furthermore, In addition, Moreover,
Comparison			In the same way, Likewise, Similarly,
Contrast	but	although while	Conversely, However, In contrast, Instead, On the other hand,
Refutation			On the contrary,
Concession	yet	although even though though	Admittedly, Despite this, Even so, Nevertheless,
Emphasis			Actually, In fact,
Clarification			In other words, In simpler words, More simply,
Reason/Cause	for	because since	
Result	so	so	As a consequence, As a result, Consequently, Therefore, Thus,
Time		after until as when as soon as while before whenever	Afterward, First, Second, Next, Then, Finally, Subsequently, Meanwhile, In the meantime,
Condition		even if unless if when provided that	
Purpose		in order that so that	
Choice	or		

APPENDIX 9 Useful Phrases

Contrasting

S + V. *In contrast,* S + V.	Algeria is a very large country. In contrast, Tunisia is very small.
Contrasted with / In contrast to NOUN, ...	In contrast to his earlier works, Goya's Black Paintings were extremely disturbing.
Although / Even though / Though S + V, ...	Though London in 1900 was quite different from London in 2000, important similarities existed in population and transportation.
Unlike NOUN, NOUN ...	Unlike the rest of the world, the United States has not adopted the metric system.
S + V. *However,* S + V.	Single-serving coffee machines are convenient. However, their packaging is bad for the environment.
On the one hand, S + V. *On the other hand,* S + V.	On the one hand, technology in the classroom can speed up the research process. On the other hand, it can be a distraction.
S + V, *yet* S + V.	People know that eating sweets is not good for their health, yet they continue to consume a great deal of sugar.
NOUN *and* NOUN *are surprisingly different.*	Finland and Iceland are surprisingly different.

Comparing

NOUN *is* COMPARATIVE ADJECTIVE *than* NOUN.	New York is larger than Rhode Island.
S + V + COMPARATIVE ADVERB *than* NOUN.	Norway extends much farther to the north than Sweden does.
S + V. *In comparison,* S + V.	The average American consumes about 120 kilograms of meat per year. In comparison, the average person in Japan consumes just 46 kilograms.
Although NOUN *and* NOUN *are similar in* NOUN, ...	Although France and Spain are similar in size, they are different in many ways.
Upon closer inspection, S + V.	Upon closer inspection, teachers in both schools discovered their students progressed faster when using games.

Comparing (continued)

Compared to …	Compared to Mexico, Puerto Rico is very densely populated.
NOUN *and* NOUN *are surprisingly similar.*	Birds and reptiles are surprisingly similar.
S + V. *The same …*	Brazil was first colonized by Portugal. The same can be said about Canada.
Like NOUN, NOUN *also …*	Like Claudius, Caesar Augustus may have also been poisoned by his wife.
Compared to …	Compared to U.S. history, Chinese history is very long.
Both NOUN *and* NOUN + V.	Both models and real planes have similar controls.
S + V. *Also / Likewise,* S + V.	The new law protects tenants from eviction. Likewise, it protects landlords from tenants who do not pay rent.
S + V. *Similarly,* S + V.	Data from 1990 showed that the number of frogs in the area was starting to increase. Similarly, recent data has confirmed that the population has grown significantly.

Showing Cause and Effect

Because S + V, …	Because their races are longer, distance runners need to be mentally as well as physically strong.
On account of / *As a result of* / *Because of* NOUN, …	On account of the economic sanctions, the unemployment rate skyrocketed.
NOUN *can cause / trigger* NOUN.	An earthquake can trigger tidal waves.
While S + V, …	While the antibiotics fight the infection, there can be terrible side effects.
S + V. *Therefore,* / *As a result,* / *For this reason,* / *Consequently,* S + V.	Markets fell. Therefore, millions of people lost their life savings.
NOUN *will bring about* NOUN.	New infectious diseases will bring about a need for more affordable treatment.
NOUN *has had a positive / negative effect on* NOUN.	Social media has had both positive and negative effects on reading comprehension.
The correlation … is clear / evident.	The correlation between smoking and lung cancer is clear.

Stating an Opinion

Without a doubt, GERUND *is* ADJECTIVE *idea / method / way.*	Without a doubt, walking to work each day is an excellent way to lose weight.
GERUND *should not be allowed.*	Texting in class should not be allowed.
There are many benefits / advantages to NOUN.	There are many benefits to regular meditation.
There are many drawbacks / disadvantages to NOUN.	There are many drawbacks to leaving electronics plugged in overnight.
NOUN *should be required / mandatory.*	Art education should be required of all high school students.
For all of these important reasons, S + V.	For all of these important reasons, the U.S. government should cease production of the penny.
Based on NOUN, S + V.	Based on the facts presented, high-fat foods should be banned from the cafeteria.

Arguing and Persuading

It is important to remember + NOUN CLAUSE.	It is important to remember that self-diagnosis is rarely accurate.
According to a recent survey, S + V.	According to a recent survey, most people's biggest fear is of making a speech in public.
Even more important, S + V.	Even more important, the printing press made the possibility of self-education a reality for the masses.
Despite this, S + V.	Despite this, most people still lacked the spare time to read.
S + *must / should / ought to* ...	Researchers must stop unethical animal testing.
For these reasons, S + V.	For these reasons, the Internet should never be governed by one specific country.
Obviously, S + V.	Obviously, citizens will get used to this new law.
Without a doubt, S + V.	Without a doubt, people with pets should not smoke indoors.
I agree that S + V; *however,* S + V	I agree that a college degree is important; however, getting a practical technical license can also be very useful.

Giving a Counterargument

Proponents / Opponents may say + NOUN CLAUSE.	Opponents of public television may say that government funds should never be used for entertainment.
On the surface this might seem logical / smart / correct; however, S + V.	On the surface this might seem logical; however, it is not an affordable solution.
S + V; *however, this is not the case.*	Most people believe that biking on the sidewalk is safer than the road; however, this is not the case.
One could argue + NOUN CLAUSE, *but* S + V.	One could argue that working in a start-up company is very exciting, but it can also be more stressful than a job in a large company.
It would be wrong to say + NOUN CLAUSE.	It would be wrong to say that nuclear energy is 100 percent safe.
Some people believe + NOUN CLAUSE.	Some people believe that nuclear energy is the way of the future.
Upon further investigation, S + V.	Upon further investigation, one begins to see why IQ tests are an incomplete measure of intelligence.
S + V. *However, I cannot agree with this idea.*	Some people think logging in our forests should be banned. However, I cannot agree with this idea.
Some people may say (one opinion), *but I believe / think / say* (opposite opinion).	Some people may say that working from home is lonely, but I believe that it is easy, productive, and rewarding.
While NOUN *has its merits,* NOUN …	While working at a company has its merits, working from home has many more benefits.
Although it is true + NOUN CLAUSE, S + V.	Although it is true that taking online classes can be convenient, it is difficult for many students to stay on task.

Reacting or Responding

TITLE *by* AUTHOR *is a / an* …	*Harry Potter and the Goblet of Fire* by J.K. Rowling is a turning point for the maturity level of the series.
My first reaction to the prompt / news / article was / is NOUN.	My first reaction to the article was fear.
When I read / looked at / thought about NOUN, *I was amazed / shocked / surprised* …	When I read the article, I was surprised to learn of his athletic ability.

Averil Coxhead (2000)

The following words are on the Academic Word List (AWL). The AWL is a list of the 570 highest-frequency academic word families that regularly appear in academic texts. The AWL was compiled by researcher Averil Coxhead based on her analysis of a 3.5-million-word corpus of academic texts and is reprinted with her permission.

abandon	assign	commit	contribute
abstract	assist	commodity	controversy
academy	assume	communicate	convene
access	assure	community	converse
accommodate	attach	compatible	convert
accompany	attain	compensate	convince
accumulate	attitude	compile	cooperate
accurate	attribute	complement	coordinate
achieve	author	complex	core
acknowledge	authority	component	corporate
acquire	automate	compound	correspond
adapt	available	comprehensive	couple
adequate	aware	comprise	create
adjacent	behalf	compute	credit
adjust	benefit	conceive	criteria
administrate	bias	concentrate	crucial
adult	bond	concept	culture
advocate	brief	conclude	currency
affect	bulk	concurrent	cycle
aggregate	capable	conduct	data
aid	capacity	confer	debate
albeit	category	confine	decade
allocate	cease	confirm	decline
alter	challenge	conflict	deduce
alternative	channel	conform	define
ambiguous	chapter	consent	definite
amend	chart	consequent	demonstrate
analogy	chemical	considerable	denote
analyze	circumstance	consist	deny
annual	cite	constant	depress
anticipate	civil	constitute	derive
apparent	clarify	constrain	design
append	classic	construct	despite
appreciate	clause	consult	detect
approach	code	consume	deviate
appropriate	coherent	contact	device
approximate	coincide	contemporary	devote
arbitrary	collapse	context	differentiate
area	colleague	contract	dimension
aspect	commence	contradict	diminish
assemble	comment	contrary	discrete
assess	commission	contrast	discriminate

displace
display
dispose
distinct
distort
distribute
diverse
document
domain
domestic
dominate
draft
drama
duration
dynamic
economy
edit
element
eliminate
emerge
emphasis
empirical
enable
encounter
energy
enforce
enhance
enormous
ensure
entity
environment
equate
equip
equivalent
erode
error
establish
estate
estimate
ethic
ethnic
evaluate
eventual
evident
evolve
exceed
exclude
exhibit
expand
expert
explicit

exploit
export
expose
external
extract
facilitate
factor
feature
federal
fee
file
final
finance
finite
flexible
fluctuate
focus
format
formula
forthcoming
found
foundation
framework
function
fund
fundamental
furthermore
gender
generate
generation
globe
goal
grade
grant
guarantee
guideline
hence
hierarchy
highlight
hypothesis
identical
identify
ideology
ignorant
illustrate
image
immigrate
impact
implement
implicate
implicit

imply
impose
incentive
incidence
incline
income
incorporate
index
indicate
individual
induce
inevitable
infer
infrastructure
inherent
inhibit
initial
initiate
injure
innovate
input
insert
insight
inspect
instance
institute
instruct
integral
integrate
integrity
intelligent
intense
interact
intermediate
internal
interpret
interval
intervene
intrinsic
invest
investigate
invoke
involve
isolate
issue
item
job
journal
justify
label
labor

layer
lecture
legal
legislate
levy
liberal
license
likewise
link
locate
logic
maintain
major
manipulate
manual
margin
mature
maximize
mechanism
media
mediate
medical
medium
mental
method
migrate
military
minimal
minimize
minimum
ministry
minor
mode
modify
monitor
motive
mutual
negate
network
neutral
nevertheless
nonetheless
norm
normal
notion
notwithstanding
nuclear
objective
obtain
obvious
occupy

occur	prohibit	route	task
odd	project	scenario	team
offset	promote	schedule	technical
ongoing	proportion	scheme	technique
option	prospect	scope	technology
orient	protocol	section	temporary
outcome	psychology	sector	tense
output	publication	secure	terminate
overall	publish	seek	text
overlap	purchase	select	theme
overseas	pursue	sequence	theory
panel	qualitative	series	thereby
paradigm	quote	sex	thesis
paragraph	radical	shift	topic
parallel	random	significant	trace
parameter	range	similar	tradition
participate	ratio	simulate	transfer
partner	rational	site	transform
passive	react	so-called	transit
perceive	recover	sole	transmit
percent	refine	somewhat	transport
period	regime	source	trend
persist	region	specific	trigger
perspective	register	specify	ultimate
phase	regulate	sphere	undergo
phenomenon	reinforce	stable	underlie
philosophy	reject	statistic	undertake
physical	relax	status	uniform
plus	release	straightforward	unify
policy	relevant	strategy	unique
portion	reluctance	stress	utilize
pose	rely	structure	valid
positive	remove	style	vary
potential	require	submit	vehicle
practitioner	research	subordinate	version
precede	reside	subsequent	via
precise	resolve	subsidy	violate
predict	resource	substitute	virtual
predominant	respond	successor	visible
preliminary	restore	sufficient	vision
presume	restrain	sum	visual
previous	restrict	summary	volume
primary	retain	supplement	voluntary
prime	reveal	survey	welfare
principal	revenue	survive	whereas
principle	reverse	suspend	whereby
prior	revise	sustain	widespread
priority	revolution	symbol	
proceed	rigid	tape	
process	role	target	
professional			